MINDFULNESS POCKETBOOK

MINDFULNESS POCKETBOOK

LITTLE EXERCISES FOR A CALMER LIFE

Gill Hasson

CAPSTONE
A Wiley Brand

Registered office

Capstone Publishing Ltd. (A Wiley Company), John Wiley and Sons Ltd, The Atrium, Southern Gate, Chichester, West Sussex, PO19 8SQ, United Kingdom

For details of our global editorial offices, for customer services and for information about how to apply for permission to reuse the copyright material in this book please see our website at www.wiley.com.

The right of the author to be identified as the author of this work has been asserted in accordance with the Copyright, Designs and Patents Act 1988.

Reprinted April 2015, June 2015, July 2015, September 2015, November 2015, February 2016, February 2017 June 2018, November 2018

Library of Congress Cataloging-in-Publication Data
Hasson, Gill.
  Mindfulness pocketbook : little exercises for a calmer life / Gill Hasson.
       pages cm
  Summary: "A step-by-step, pocket-sized guide to achieving a more manageable life. Packed with exercises, practices, and reflective tools of Mindfulness, this little book combines simple everyday wisdom with practical, implementable ways to develop balance and harmony in all areas of life"– Provided by publisher.
  ISBN 978-0-85708-589-4 (paperback)
  1. Stress management.   2. Mind and body.   I. Title.
  RA785.H377 2015
  613—dc23

                                                                                          2014045119

A catalogue record for this book is available from the British Library.

ISBN 978-0-857-08589-4 (pbk) ISBN 978-0-857-08590-0 (ebk)
ISBN 978-0-857-08591-7 (ebk)

Cover Design and Illustration: Wiley
Set in 10/12.5pt, RotisSansSerifStd by Laserwords Private Limited, Chennai, India

Printed in Great Britain by TJ International Ltd, Padstow, Cornwall, UK

For Gilly, Janine, Karen, Jenny and Donna;
for all the fun and all the mindful moments.

CONTENTS

INTRODUCTION

'How we spend our days is, of course, how we spend our lives.' – Annie Dillard

What is it with mindfulness? Why is there such interest, such a buzz, around mindfulness?

Too often, life zips by. There's no time to experience what's happening now, because you're busy thinking about what needs doing tomorrow or you're caught up with thoughts about what did or didn't happen yesterday. Your mind is chattering with commentary or judgement.

But thinking is not the enemy. It's essential to your life. Your mind is able to think back and reflect on past events and experiences and learn from those experiences, and you can reflect with pleasure on the good times. Your mind can also think about the future. It can plan ahead and look forward to forthcoming events.

This ability to think back to the past and forward to the future is not, though, always a blessing. Your mind's ability to project backwards and forwards means that you can get stuck in the past, going back over and dwelling on events. You can also be paralysed by worries and anxiety about the future.

Mindfulness is a way to have a more helpful relationship with this thinking, to recognize when your thoughts are being unhelpfully dragged back to the past or catapulted into the future. Mindfulness is about knowing where you are (being in the moment) but also having an awareness of – but not getting stuck in – where you have been (reflection) and where you are going (anticipating).

But how can mindfulness be helpful in your everyday life – as you go to and from work, in your job, with your family and friends, with cooking and eating and even sleeping?

Many of us work in a fast-paced, stressful world, dealing with a flood of information including email, meetings, text messages, phone calls, interruptions and distractions at work. Family life can also be fast paced and stressful – managing a job, a home and the variety of demands as you try to meet everyone's needs and your own commitments. Thinking about what needs doing and what you didn't do, getting frustrated, stressed and anxious.

Unfortunately, a good part of our time passes that way for most of us. We're in one place doing one thing but thinking of things we aren't doing and places we aren't at.

It's easy to stop noticing what's really going on within you and around you – your surroundings and other people – and to end up living in your head, caught up in your thoughts without being aware of how those thoughts are controlling what you feel and do. It's easy to waste 'now' time, missing what is happening in the only moment that really exists.

Mindfulness enables you to experience and appreciate your life instead of rushing through it, constantly trying to be somewhere else. Mindfulness is not another set of instructions. Mindfulness is simply a shift in your awareness of your life – your routines and habits, work and relationships.

HOW TO USE THIS BOOK

'Start where you are. Use what you have. Do what you can.' – Arthur Ashe

If you can be present and in the moment sitting in a quiet room then why not when you're eating a meal, drinking a cup of tea, travelling to and from your job, being at work, working at the computer or in your relationships with family, friends and colleagues?

There are many ways in which you can practise mindfulness and many ways in which you can anchor yourself to any given moment.

Throughout this book, you will come across five recurring themes:

 Mindful qualities.

Mindful work.

Mindful body and mind.

Mindful relationships.

Mindful eating.

Within each theme, you'll find a particular situation or circumstance where mindfulness is useful and where there are opportunities to be mindful. Alongside this, you will find practical ways – ideas, tips, techniques and suggestions – to be mindful and to use mindfulness.

You'll see that the aspects and qualities of mindfulness – awareness, acknowledgement and acceptance, focus and engagement, beginner's mind, letting go and being non-judgemental – are both a separate theme with their own pages and principles that appear throughout this book. Each time you apply these principles, each time you apply an aspect of mindfulness, you are learning how to relate more directly to your life.

Whether you need tips, techniques, ideas and suggestions or just a simple quote to inspire you, this book will help. Keep it in your bag or your pocket to inspire you whenever or wherever mindfulness can help slow things down, provide perspective and a sense of calm control in the moment and moments of your life.

CREATING A MINDFULNESS HABIT

'Habit is a cable; we weave a thread each day, and at last we cannot break it.'
– Horace Mann

It isn't necessary to be mindful in all your waking hours, but unless you make a concerted effort to be mindful on a daily basis it's easy to get distracted by myriad things that divert your attention through the day.

Occasional attempts at 'being in the moment' or to 'notice the little things more' and 'live in the now' are well meaning, but distractions and preoccupations take over and resolutions to be more mindful fall by the wayside.

What to do? You need to make mindfulness a habit, something that you do on a regular basis until it becomes your normal, everyday practice.

Your mind *is* able to do this!

Establishing new ways of thinking and doing is not difficult, provided the new ways are constantly repeated. How come? When you think or do something in a new way, you create new connections, or neural pathways, in your brain. Then, every time you repeat that thought or action, every time you continue using these new pathways, they become stronger and more established.

It's like walking through a field of long grass, each step helps to create a new path and every time you walk that new path you establish a clear route which becomes easier to use each time. It becomes a habit to use that route.

Since your distracted and preoccupied mind isn't going to remind you to be mindful, you need something else to remind you.

In Practice

'The hard must become habit. The habit must become easy. The easy must become beautiful.' – Doug Henning

Set a timer on your phone (with a soothing tone) to remind you to be mindful at random times of your day. A 'Mindfulness Bell' app is useful here. It rings periodically during the day to give you the opportunity to pause for a moment and consider where you are, what you are doing and what you are thinking.

Put a note on your bathroom mirror saying: 'Be mindful.'

Decide to do things differently to experience different results. Write them on self-sticking notes and place them on the wall above your desk or on the fridge to remind you to do things differently.

Make a mindfulness date with yourself, a time in your day when you do something specifically devoted to mindfulness. It could be taking a short walk, eating a quiet meal or drinking a cup of tea.

Commit to being mindful every time you open a door. When you open a door, drop what's in your mind (you can pick it up again shortly) and, instead, watch your hand push the door or grasp the doorknob. Open the door with purpose and patience. Feel its weight and whether it opens easily. Take in the new scene that's revealed. Smell the air and notice any change in temperature of the outside space or room you are entering. Listen to the sound of the space you've just left, give way to the room or space you've just entered.

It's a small commitment, maybe five seconds at a time, a handful of times a day.

Just be sure that when you open a door, you *open the door*. You're going to do it anyway. Make it an opportunity to be present.

BRINGING OUT YOUR CONFIDENCE

'It's not who you are that holds you back, it's who you think you're not.'
– Denis Waitley

Do you feel that life would improve for you if you had more self-confidence?

When faced with a new challenge or opportunity, are you filled with self-doubt? Do you say to yourself, 'I'll never be able to do this' or 'I'm not good enough' or 'I can't'?

Self-confidence is not about what you can or can't do: it's what you *believe* you can or can't do.

If, in the past, you've failed or not coped well with a particular situation, you may well *believe* that you will fail or struggle the next time. You won't feel confident about doing it again.

And if you've now got something you have to do, something new you've never done before, you may *believe* you won't be able to do it. You won't feel confident about your ability to do it. So if you lack self-confidence, you'll avoid taking risks and stretching yourself and will probably not try at all.

You'll talk yourself out of it with negative self-talk, telling yourself that you can't or won't be able to do something. You will make yourself *believe* that you can't do certain things. (Negative self-talk also knocks your self-esteem, making you feel bad about yourself.)

Instead of letting past experience or future possibilities paralyse you, mindfulness can help you be aware of these judgemental thoughts and how unhelpful they are.

In Practice

'Accept your past without regret, handle your present with confidence and face your future without fear.' – Unknown

Get yourself into a positive mindset. Remind yourself of the things that you do well, activities where you feel a sense of control, no fear of failure or feeling of self-consciousness. You know what you're doing and where you're heading: you feel confident in your abilities.

When you find yourself basing your beliefs about your abilities on what happened in the past, start again. Take a 'beginner's mind' approach: put the past judgements and conclusions aside and, instead, think about what you've learnt from these experiences. You can't change what happened last time you did something, but you can change what happens next time. Identify new insights that could help you do things differently next time.

Make a plan. If you're faced with a new challenge or situation, something you've never done before, think through what steps you can take to manage potential difficulties.

Know that when you stop giving the situation any more unhelpful thoughts – thoughts based on the past and the future – you will have taken the first step towards moving ahead with confidence.

Use mindfulness to catch yourself when you think, 'I can't do this.' There's no need to judge yourself for having unhelpful thoughts. Just notice and make a different choice. Choose to think, 'I *can* do this. I've thought it through. I have a plan.'

CARRYING YOURSELF WITH CONFIDENCE

'I speak two languages. Body and English.'
– Mae West

Do you remember the last time you had an interview or important meeting or had to give a presentation? The last time you went to a party where you hardly knew anyone there? A time when you had to stand up to someone else?

Were you aware of your body language: your posture, facial expressions and gestures?

Perhaps your mind was too preoccupied with what to do, what to say and how to say it to think about body language. Or perhaps, you may have been overly conscious, too aware of what message your body language may have been sending to other people.

But have you ever considered what message your body language might be sending to your own brain?

Recent research suggests that the way you sit or stand can actually affect the way your brain functions. Carry yourself with confidence and in a matter of minutes, the chemical balance – the testosterone and cortisol levels in the brain – alters, your body starts to feel it and your brain starts to believe it.

So, by being aware of and focusing on just one or two aspects of your body language, you can directly influence the message your brain will receive.

You don't have to learn a new repertoire of poses, gestures and expressions that feel unnatural or uncomfortable. If you can alter just one or two things consistently, the rest of your body and mind will catch up and you will feel more confident and come across as more confident and capable.

In Practice

'Our bodies change our minds, and our minds can change our behaviour, and our behaviour can change our outcomes.' – Amy Cuddy

If you want to feel calmer, more confident and in the moment – not just appear confident but genuinely feel confident – simply choose to do just two or three of these actions:

- Stand or sit straight.
- Keep your head level.
- Relax your shoulders.
- Spread your weight evenly on both legs.
- If sitting, keep your elbows on the arms of your chair (rather than tightly against your sides).
- Make appropriate eye contact.
- Lower the pitch of your voice.
- Speak more slowly.

You can't control *all* your non-verbal communication. In fact, the harder you try, the more unnatural you are likely to feel. But if you can keep your mind on doing one or two of those things consistently, your thoughts, feelings and behaviour can match up. Which one or two actions would you feel comfortable using? Practise using them right now!

Adopt a 'Mona Lisa' smile. A 'Mona Lisa' smile is helpful in stressful situations because it is an easy way to be in the moment and create a feeling of calm. The Mona Lisa's smile is an almost imperceptible smile: you simply relax your jaw and let your mouth turn slightly upward at the ends. It can help to visualize the image of the Mona Lisa. Or imagine yourself looking into a mirror with a half-smile. The 'Mona Lisa' smile can be used with your breathing. Inhale the calm. Exhale with a half-smile.

DEVELOPING YOUR ABILITY TO 'READ' OTHERS

'The face is more honest than the mouth will ever be.'
– Daphne Orebaugh

How good are you at mind reading? How good are you at knowing what someone is thinking or feeling without their having to tell you? You're probably pretty good at it. You can get better.

When you observe a person's body language, you can see what they are feeling and thinking as they feel and think it. If, for example, you see their face is contorted and they are banging their fist on the table, you know that person is angry.

Facial expressions, posture, touch etc. are all emotionally driven and can clue you into a person's true feelings and intentions in any one moment. Every shift in a person's inner emotions is communicated through their non-verbal behaviour and it happens in the present.

However, not all emotions are as obvious and easy to read as anger or joy. Disappointment, for example, is expressed in far more subtle ways than anger. It's not so easy to read what's going on.

Many emotions occur fleetingly – they happen in the moment – so you need to pay attention. By mindfully observing people as they communicate, you are more likely to notice those subtle fleeting cues as they happen. You can get a real insight into what's going on for that person, in that moment.

In Practice

'The physical language of the body is so much more powerful than the words.' – Bill Irwin

Practise your ability to 'read' other people. Observe people on a bus, train, in a café and just notice how they act and react to each other. When you watch others, try to guess what they are saying or get a sense of what is going on between them.

Watch interviews, dramas and documentaries on TV. Turn the sound down and try to guess what emotions people are experiencing and displaying as they interact with each other.

Look for a combination of expressions and gestures in any one moment. A single expression or gesture isn't as reliable as two or three body language signals. If, for example, they were frowning, closing their eyes and rubbing their head, you would probably conclude that they have a headache. Together, two or three signals more clearly indicate what's going on in that moment.

Notice if what someone says matches or if it is at odds with their non-verbal behaviour.

Pay attention to changes in body language. Every shift in a person's emotions is conveyed through their non-verbal behaviour.

KEEPING ON TOP WHEN THE PRESSURE IS ON

'You can do anything but not everything.'
– David Allen

Think of a typical busy day at work, study or at home. What time is it? What are you doing? What are you thinking? What do you have to do next? What haven't you done? How do you feel?

At one time or another most of us experience busy periods at work, with study or home life. There's much to do and much to think about. You're doing several things at once and life just races by.

You're caught up with what you haven't done and what you've yet to do and your mind is chattering away with judgements and commentary. You feel anxious, frustrated, overwhelmed and stressed. It's impossible to think clearly.

How does this happen? It's all in the mind!

There are two important parts to your brain: the limbic system and the neocortex. The limbic system in your brain is responsible for your emotions, emotions such as agitation, frustration and disappointment which can overwhelm your mind. You react to what's happening instinctively, without rational thought or reasoning. More so when you're busy or under pressure.

The neocortex is responsible for thinking, remembering and reasoning. Focus and attention are primarily activities of the neocortex.

Mindfulness can calm unhelpful activity from the limbic system. Your mind becomes quieter. You can think more clearly and deliberately, bring yourself back to the present and just stay with what's happening now.

In Practice

'If you want to conquer the anxiety of life, live in the moment, live in the breath.' – Amit Ray

Acknowledge and accept the feeling of being overwhelmed. This doesn't mean you have to accept and resign yourself to difficult, stressful situations. You simply accept how you feel and how things are at this moment before thinking about what you can do to manage them. It's a strategic acceptance. You may not like what's happening but, instead of fighting it, by accepting it you can engage the reasoning, thinking part of your brain and find a solution.

Get some breathing space. You can do this anywhere at any time. Simply take two or three minutes to stop what you're doing and focus on breathing. A two-minute breathing space will help calm you down, collect and clarify your thoughts. It helps you to engage the rationalizing reasoning part of your brain.

During busy, stressful periods, try to get some breathing space two or three times a day.

Breaks give your mind space to digest, mentally process and assimilate what's happening internally and externally. You don't need to try to do it consciously. It's something that the brain just does naturally below the surface.

USING YOUR BREATH

'Feelings come and go like clouds in a windy sky. Conscious breathing is my anchor.' – Thich Nhất Hạnh

Breathing is the foundation of mindfulness. It can help slow everything down, calm your mind and body and bring you into the present moment.

There are a number of ways you can focus on your breath – you can start by being aware that, just like the ocean waves, your breaths come and go. Each time you breathe out, you can let go and release your thoughts about the past and future. Just focus on breathing in ... then breathing out. That's mindful breathing.

You will notice thoughts arising as you breathe. Let them come and go and return your focus and attention to your breathing.

Mindful breathing is like a reset button you can push to return yourself to the present moment whenever you feel the need, an effective way of orienting yourself to the now, not because the breath has some magical property but because it's always there with you.

Try to practise mindful breathing for a minute or two a few times each day. It could be before you get dressed in the morning, on the journey to work, with a cup of tea, at lunch or before you get ready for bed.

There are a number of ways you can keep focused on breathing. Try them and see which one you prefer – which ones are the most doable for you? Wondering which breathing technique to use is not as important as just remembering to use one of them!

In Practice

'When you own your breath, nobody can steal your peace.' – Unknown

Feel your breathing. Place one hand on your chest and feel your breath moving into and out of your body. Notice the natural rhythm. Be aware of the coolness of the air as you breathe in and the warmth of the air leaving you as you exhale.

Breathe slowly and deeply. Start by breathing normally, then, every few breaths, inhale through your nose slowly to a count of five. Pause and hold your breath for a count of three then breathe out slowly, blowing out air through your mouth. When you've exhaled completely, take two breaths in your normal rhythm, and then repeat the cycle. It's just like you're smoking a cigarette. But without the cigarette.

Alternate your breathing. Push one nostril closed with your finger. Take one long breath in through the open nostril and then pinch that one and let go of the other, breathing out slowly. Repeat alternately. Try to breathe out for as long as possible.

Use your imagination. Breathe in like you're smelling the scent of a flower. Breathe out like you're blowing bubbles. Or imagine breathing out to the ends of the universe and breathing from there back into your body. Or breathe colour: imagine the colour of the air filling not just your lungs but also your entire body.

Count backwards. Inhale deeply. When you breathe out, count backwards from nine: nine, eight, seven, six and so on. On the next breath, when you breathe out, count backwards from eight. With the next breath, count backwards from seven. And so on, adjusting the length of time you breathe in and out according to which number you are counting backwards from.

MANAGING INTERRUPTIONS

'You will never reach your destination if you stop to throw stones at every dog that barks.' – Winston Churchill

Mindfulness involves managing your attention so that it is focused and occupied with immediate experience. What usually stops you from focusing and engaging at work? Interruptions and distractions.

Interruptions arrive unexpectedly at any time of day. They come from other people in the form of questions, announcements, requests and demands, by people who need decisions made, conflicts managed and problems solved. Interruptions come in person, by phone, texts and email.

Interruptions get in the way of managing your time and your work. They disturb, delay and hinder you. Interruptions deplete your time and energy. They break your concentration and cause delays.

Because your day only has so many hours in it, a handful of small interruptions can rob you of the time you need to get on with and complete your work. Interruptions can break your focus, meaning that you have to spend time re-engaging your brain with the thought processes needed to complete your work.

Interruptions may feel like they are not in your control but they *can* be managed.

In Practice

'Focusing is about saying no.' – Steve Jobs

Accept that interruptions will happen. Then plan for them – leave gaps in your day for interruptions and so prevent them from frustrating you.

Set criteria for other people interrupting you, so that only decisions above a certain threshold of importance will come to you. If someone interrupts you with a query you think needs discussion, tell them you will get back to them later, when you'll give it your full attention.

Set times to be available. Other people will interrupt you only if they know it's okay to interrupt you at any time and that you will respond.

Set times that you are available to deal with their problems and questions. For example, tell people that you only check email at 3 p.m. because you need to focus on other work. Then you can deal with problems/ requests at certain times of the day, and focus during other times.

Delegate. If you're in a supervisory or managerial position, when all queries and decisions must come through you, it's inevitable that you're going to be interrupted. So train others to make these decisions. Set guidelines for making decisions so they'd make pretty much the same as you in any given situation.

Learn to say no. Be assertive. Learn to say no (nicely) to requests or tasks if you are busy, if someone else can handle it, if it is not an important task or if it can be done later.

Be patient. If you can't avoid interruptions, deal with each interruption one at a time. Give your full attention to each person and each query or problem. This way, you will be less stressed and will deal calmly and fully with every person who needs your attention.

BEING SPIRITUALLY AWARE

'Just as a candle cannot burn without fire, we cannot live without a spiritual life.' – Buddha

Spirituality: we all have some sort of vision in mind when we hear the word 'spirituality'. Maybe it's an image of a group of monks living a simple life in a faraway place. Perhaps it's a vision of someone wandering down a mythological spiritual path on their 'spiritual journey'.

With mindfulness, there is no spiritual path, because there is no need to go anywhere. You're already there. You just haven't realized it.

Quite simply, spirituality is a sense of being part of something bigger, more eternal than the physical and yourself.

Like many of the world's religions, spirituality is an awareness of and a relationship with something that connects you to a purpose in life larger than yourself.

You don't have to be religious to be spiritual. Even if you regard yourself as an atheist, you can feel a sense of connection from contemplating a beautiful sunset or the power of the sea.

Spirituality helps you to be mindful because it can anchor you and give you perspective – to be aware of where you are and how you're connected in the greater scheme of things.

You can choose to define what that means for you, in whatever way feels most appropriate. Your own sense of spirituality can be experienced by anything from cheering your team along with ten thousand other people to something as simple as gazing at a star-filled sky.

Spirituality helps you to feel grounded in the present and connected to the past and the future.

In Practice

'The fact that I can plant a seed and it becomes a flower, share a bit of knowledge and it becomes another's, smile at someone and receive a smile in return are to me continual spiritual exercises.' – Leo Buscaglia

Raise your awareness. Think about what you *already* do that makes you feel connected. Perhaps it's playing a team sport, singing in a choir, gardening, being at a music festival.

Get connected. Support and become active in an organization with a cause you believe in. Organizations such as Amnesty International, Save the Children or the World Wildlife Fund can connect you to other people and unite you in a common purpose. Or find a local charity that interests you, maybe one that promotes arts and culture or environmental concerns or works with children and young people. The positivity and sense of connection that can be gained from helping other people are key aspects of spirituality.

Learn to appreciate the beauty of what we are naturally a part of, concepts such as: music and art, wildlife and the miracles of nature.

Find someone who is spiritual. Who do you already know who has balance and a sense of perspective, who has a calm concern and rapport with other people? It could be someone with a sense of wonder, someone who seeks out beauty and peace in the things they do. Spend time with spiritual people you admire. Their attitude will inspire you.

LISTENING INSTEAD OF JUST HEARING

'The first duty of love is to listen.' – Paul Tillich

Is listening the same as hearing? No. There is a difference. If you hear something, you are simply *aware* of sound; you don't have to make any effort to receive the sounds. You can do and think about other things and still be able to hear what's going on around you and what other people are saying.

Listening, on the other hand, requires you to concentrate. Mindful listening takes things one step further. It focuses your attention: you closely follow what someone is saying.

Instead of half listening and thinking about something else or what you're going to say next, with mindful listening you are completely present and tuned in.

Mindful listening helps to create connections with others. It increases understanding, interest and rapport between you and other people, with friends, family and colleagues.

Learn to listen mindfully and you will improve your relationships with others.

In Practice

'Think of listening as a form of meditation. Quiet your mind and focus your attention on listening.' – Linda Eve Diamond

Practise mindful reflective listening with a friend or colleague. One of you talk for two minutes on one of the subjects listed below. (If you can't practise with someone else, listen to someone talking on the radio or a podcast for a few minutes.)

- The best job or holiday you ever had.
- The worst job or holiday you ever had.
- How you would spend five million pounds.
- The weirdest dream you ever had.
- Which three famous people you would join for dinner. Why?

When the person has finished speaking, the listener must summarize or paraphrase what the speaker said. Repeat in your own words your understanding of what the other person said.

What were the main points of what they said? What feelings were apparent?

Of course, it would be quite odd to repeat or paraphrase what you heard every time someone spoke to you!

The crucial thing is to listen as if you were going to reflect back. Whether you do so or not. This is why *mindful listening* is so powerful. It focuses your attention, helps *you* to listen, be aware of feelings and encourages further communication.

HAVING A BEGINNER'S MIND

'Be willing to be a beginner every single morning.' – Meister Eckhart

Having a 'beginner's mind' simply means that you engage with other people, events, objects and activities as if for the first time.

Usually, what you do, how you think and how you feel are based on past experience, beliefs, judgements and conclusions. But when you do things the same way and take the same route as you have done before, when you stick to your habitual ways of thinking and responding to events and other people, you miss all sorts of possibilities, discoveries and insights. You are taking a narrow path that makes it less likely that you will come across new ideas and ways of seeing and understanding.

Rather than respond to events, experiences, places and other people in the same old ways – ways from the past – beginner's mind encourages you to take a new perspective and to respond to things as they are right now.

Beginner's mind doesn't dismiss or devalue your past knowledge and experience. It simply suggests you keep an open mind on how to apply your experience to each and every situation.

Beginner's mind can help you to slow down, to experience life in the present moment, because you are looking to notice something new in a situation. It puts you in the here and now because you have a heightened awareness to what's happening right now.

This makes life interesting and fresh. It keeps you alert, aware and keen to learn.

In Practice

Take a different route. Is there a journey you take on a regular basis? Try leaving ten minutes earlier and taking a different route. Taking a different route allows/encourages you to engage/notice new things.

You can even try this at the supermarket. If you have a route that you normally take around the supermarket aisles, change the route. Yes, it will slow you down but you never know what new foods and products you will discover!

Listen to music differently. With a beginner's mind, you can listen to familiar pieces of music as if for the first time. Choose a favourite piece of music. Pick out an element that you don't usually listen to – the beat, the melody, the lyrics or a particular instrument. Now listen to and follow the music, focusing on the new element you have chosen. Even though you may have listened to this music many times before, when you listen with a beginner's mind, you experience it anew. You are in the moment.

Learn something new. It could simply be a new recipe but it could also mean learning a new skill – a language, creative writing, bricklaying or drawing. It could be a sport – tennis or badminton. Learning something new is the definitive way of having a beginner's mind because you really are starting at the beginning.

See someone in a different light. Think of someone you have always found difficult to get on with – a family member or a colleague, for example. Put aside your beliefs and opinions about them and see something new about them. Look for something positive. It could be an aspect of their personality, their attitude, something about the way they interact with others or something about how they work.

SLOWING DOWN

'There is more to life than increasing its speed.' – Gandhi

Technological inventions are continually saving you time: your car gets you there quicker than walking, the microwave cooker heats up your food in seconds, Internet shopping saves you going to the shops, Internet banking saves you time from actually going to the bank and so on.

What do you do with all that time spared? Like many of us, you probably use it to fit more things into your day, and so your life is more hurried and hectic than ever.

But doing too much is not an effective way to work or live. Moving quickly may make you less effective in completing a task and can be stressful. Slowing down is a calmer and more peaceful way to approach your work.

Take time to do what you're doing instead of constantly looking for ways to save time so that you can fit more in. If you fill your day with things to do, you will always be trying to get ahead of yourself, and that's not mindful.

Instead of trying to cram too much into every day, move at a slower, more relaxed pace and get the most out of what you're doing now.

Slowing down is not always easy. Perhaps you tell yourself you just can't, your job won't allow it or you'll let people down if you don't keep up with all your commitments.

Slowing down takes practice, but it helps you focus on what you are doing and what is happening.

In Practice

'Slow down and enjoy life. It's not only the scenery you miss by going too fast – you also miss the sense of where you're going and why.' – Eddie Cantor

Do less. Prioritize: work out what's important, what really needs to be done. Do one thing at a time and let go of what's not important.

Do it in slow motion. Whatever you're doing at the moment, slow it down by 25 per cent, whether it's typing on a keyboard, surfing the Internet, making a cup of tea or cleaning the house. Take your time. If you do less, you can do those things more slowly, more completely and with more concentration. Take your time, and move slowly. Make your actions deliberate, not rushed and random.

Breathe. When you find yourself speeding up, pause and take a deep breath. Then take a couple more.

Give yourself more time. If you're constantly rushing to appointments or other places you have to be, it's simply because you don't allot enough time. If you think it only takes you 30 minutes to get somewhere, perhaps give yourself 45 minutes so you can go at a leisurely pace and not get stressed if delays occur on the way.

Make some space. Don't plan things close together. Instead, leave room between activities and tasks. That makes your day more flexible, and leaves space in case one thing takes longer than you planned.

Reduce your commitments. Stop overcommitting yourself at work, with friends, family, hobbies and interests. Learn how to say no.

Choose a few essential commitments, and realize that the rest, while nice or important, just don't fit right now. Let other people down gently – tell them you are letting go of some of your commitments.

GAINING A SENSE OF PERSPECTIVE

'Perspective is everything when you are experiencing the challenges of life.'
– Joni Eareckson Tada

When a problem or challenge happens in your life, when major life changes come along, life becomes uncertain. In fact, you may be at a total loss as to what to do next.

Gaining perspective can help. Gaining perspective means being able to see the interrelationship between what's happening within your world and what's happening outside it. It means getting a sense of where you are in the scheme of things, taking everything else into account.

If, for example, you fail an exam, perspective helps you to understand that, as difficult to manage as it is right now, the situation will change: life will continue and things will work out.

A sense of perspective often makes the difference between resisting or accepting the changes that are happening in your life. Perspective can give you a state of calm where, right now, you can rest without needing things to be different. This doesn't mean you have to resign yourself to something, to give in. It means understanding that at this moment something is what it is.

You may want things to be different in the future, but in the present moment you accept things as they are and for what they are, knowing that this too *will* pass.

In Practice

'I see the big picture. Everything is in perspective now. Let's just say I'm the kind of guy who knows how to enjoy the moment.' – John Sununu

Ask someone over the age of 70 about their life. What went well and what didn't? Understand that they also had feelings of fear, sadness and struggle, just like you have right now. How did things turn out for them? How do they now view some of those problems when viewed in relation to everything else that happened in their life? Be aware that right now you are the one living the life you will speak of when you are older.

Read about other people's lives. *Water for Elephants* by Sara Gruen is a partial narrative by a 93-year-old man looking back at his days in the circus during the Great Depression. *Tuesdays with Morrie* by Mitch Albom tells the true story of a man who looks up his former university professor and listens to stories about his life.

Gaze at the stars. The particles of light have travelled across millions of miles, often for billions of years through space. In the moment you 'see' a star, those particles of light are being absorbed by your eyes and, in a very real sense, you have touched that age-old faraway star.

When you look up at the stars, you know you are small. But you are also big because you are connected to the stars and the stars are connected to you.

Try a spot of cloud spotting. From the fluffy cumulus to the cirrocumulus clouds that make up the patterns of a mackerel sky, there's an endless variety of clouds, and their fleeting beauty reminds you that all things will pass.

FINDING A WAY TO FORGIVE

'When you forgive, you in no way change the past – but you sure do change the future.' – Bernard Meltzer

Most of us regularly forgive other people: the person who held up the queue at the supermarket, the driver who failed to notice that the light had turned green ten seconds ago, the friend who forgot to bring wine for dinner.

These sorts of things are easy to forgive and forget. But what if you are faced with more serious issues? It's not always easy to accept what happened and forgive the other person or people involved. It can also be just as difficult to forgive yourself for something you regret having done (or not having done).

As far as mindfulness is concerned, all the time you are unable to forgive, you are living in the past. You are holding onto something that happened days, weeks, months or even years ago.

Forgiveness means letting go of the resentment, frustration or anger that you feel as a result of your own or someone else's actions. It involves no longer wanting punishment, revenge or compensation.

Forgiveness is, first and foremost, for your benefit, not the person who hurt or offended you. It means recognizing that you have already been hurt once. You do not need to let the offence, the hurt and pain burden you by holding onto it. You deserve to be free of this negativity.

If you have reached a point where you want to put your own or someone else's actions behind you and move on with your life then mindfulness can help.

In Practice

'Holding a grudge over someone is painful, but holding over yourself is the worst. Learn to forgive yourself, not just other people.' – Robin Williams

If you find yourself confronted and overwhelmed by painful memories, accept and acknowledge how you feel. Ground yourself by using mindful breathing to help you to manage the moment.

Accept what has happened and let go. No doubt, the other person (or yourself) is responsible for their actions and you wish that what they (or you) did had never happened. But you can't change what has already happened. It is what it is.

Instead of thinking about how you can get back at the other person, think about what you learnt from the experience. What would you do differently to avoid becoming involved in a similar situation?

Change the story you replay to yourself and to other people. Each time you think about what happened, each time you tell the story from the past, you relive it in the present. Change your story to one that tells of your courageous choice to let go, forgive, learn from what happened and move on.

Be patient. Give yourself time to heal. Know that letting go, acceptance and forgiveness are all part of a process. Sometimes, your ability to forgive will come quickly and easily. At other times, it will take longer.

TAKING MOUTHFULS OF MINDFULNESS

'One of the very nicest things about life is the way we must regularly stop whatever it is we are doing and devote our attention to eating.' – Luciano Pavarotti

What to eat and what not to eat? Which new diet to follow? What are the latest must-have superfoods? There is plenty of discussion about what we should or should not be eating but much less attention is paid to the question of how we eat it.

Mindful eating is not so concerned with the 'right' or 'wrong' foods and how much to eat. Mindful eating is concerned with *how* we eat.

So often, we either shovel food into our mouths without paying any attention to what we're eating and whether we feel full or obsess over what we should or shouldn't eat. Mindful eating is not directed by charts and scales and it's not dictated by an 'expert'. It's guided by you. You are the expert. In the process of learning to eat mindfully, you replace any 'food guilt' you may have with curiosity, nurturing and respect for your own wisdom.

Finding ways to slow down and eat and drink intentionally – ways that fit with your lifestyle – are part of developing a truly healthy relationship with food.

Mindful eating simply aims to reconnect you more deeply with the experience of eating and drinking – and enjoying – your food. Mindful eating is a way to rediscover one of the most pleasurable things we do as human beings.

In Practice

'The secret to staying young is to live honestly, eat slowly and lie about your age.' – Lucille Ball

Find out about the Slow Food movement (www.slowfood.org.uk), which was founded as an antidote to the rise of fast food and fast life. It supports good food, the enjoyment of eating and a slow pace of life.

Eat slowly. Practise slowing down by swapping over your knife and fork or using chopsticks. When you take the time to enjoy your food you are more likely to notice flavours and textures and be more aware of when you are full.

Savour the silence. Eat a quiet meal or snack when you can enjoy it alone. Or, when there's limited opportunity for a mindful meal, simply enjoy a cup of tea in complete silence. Just a cup of tea can be a deep meditation.

Create a tasting menu. Get together with a group of friends and create your own tasting menu. Choose a theme – Mexican, French, vegetarian or street food. Serve small portions of each prepared dish. Discuss where the ingredients came from, the smells, textures and flavours.

Hold a wine-tasting evening with friends. Be aware of:

- Aromas and flavours: What flavour or aroma comes to mind? Apple, lemon, chocolate, blackcurrant?
- Texture and weight: See if the wine is light and crisp, full-bodied, rough or smooth.
- Balance: Does the wine have a smooth mixture of flavours, or does one flavour, such as oak or tannins, dominate?
- The finish: See if the wine lingers on your palate or if it disappears the second you swallow it.

ACKNOWLEDGING AND BEING AWARE

'Awareness allows us to get outside of our mind and observe it in action.'
– Dan Brulé

You may have heard of the term 'mindful awareness' and wondered what it is you're meant to be aware *of*.

Mindful awareness simply requires you to choose (something) to notice. Once you do that, mindful awareness will follow. If, for example, you were asked to look out for anything blue, anything that colour would stand out.

You'll have experienced this awareness if you've bought a car or a baby buggy: you start noticing cars and buggies of the same make and model as the one you've just bought. The number of that type of car or buggy hasn't increased, but your awareness of it has.

Mindful awareness depends on being open and receptive to what's going on within you and around you – to thoughts and feelings, experiences, events and objects.

Mindful awareness also requires you to *acknowledge* what's happening, to consciously recognize the existence of something, recognizing thoughts, feelings and experiences as events that are occurring.

The more you notice about what's happening in and around you right now, the more in the moment you are. And being more aware helps you to appreciate what you normally take for granted and to notice when things are new or different.

In Practice

'Let us not look back in anger, nor forward in fear, but around in awareness.' – James Thurber

Listen. Each morning when you wake up, lie for a minute or two being aware of the sounds you hear. Listen to the sounds inside: your breathing, a ticking clock, other people and children moving around, talking. Be aware of the outside: traffic, people, birds, the wind or rain.

Get into the habit of being mindful of your surroundings. Look for changes in the environment on your way to work, taking children to school and so on. What's different? Describe in your head or out loud what you are seeing or doing.

If you resolve to be more aware, you'll see that almost everything is different each time: the weather, the pattern of light on the buildings, the faces of the people.

Notice small details in your environment and daily life. Use waiting time – at the traffic lights, in the doctor's waiting room – to notice something new.

Make yourself more aware by doing something new. Try a new soap or shampoo, coffee or cereal.

Move the clock or bin in your office. At home, put the jam, tea or coffee in a different cupboard. Why? Because just having to think about these things every time you go to use them will make you more aware.

Be curious. Take a photo of a building or a view every day for a week. What's different? The weather? The pattern of the light? The sky? Take a new photo of a tree every week for a year. Look for changes.

 # OPTIMIZING YOUR TIME

'Who forces time is pushed back by time; who yields to time finds time on his side.' – The Talmud

Many time management tips don't work. Some are inefficient or only useful in certain situations. Some seem to work well for other people but not for you.

Is there a way to manage your time that *does* work for you? Yes. What can help is to know your optimal times of the day. These are when your physical energy and concentration levels are at a maximum and conditions are at their best.

Some tasks (e.g. studying or writing bids) need all your focus and concentration. However, it's not a good use of time and energy if you try to do these things at a time of day that doesn't work for you. Attempt a task when your mind is wandering and the law of diminishing returns kicks in: each minute of effort produces fewer and fewer results.

That's because trying to get something done at your least-optimal time of day takes more and more effort, energy and concentration, with the result that things end up being done badly or not at all. It's difficult to be mindful – focused and engaged – because you're more easily distracted.

Conversely, getting things done at your *most* optimal time of day will take less effort and energy because it's easier to be present: focus and concentrate on what's happening and what needs doing.

It's all very well planning what you need to do but you also need to take your physical and mental focus and energy into account.

In Practice

'The bad news is time flies. The good news is you're the pilot.' – Michael Altshuler

Optimize your time. Decide whether you're a morning, afternoon or evening person. If you're not sure, try out different times of day and different amounts of time on various activities to see when you have the most mental and physical energy.

Work out what's the optimal amount of time you can focus on different tasks and activities. Experiment. It may be that you're best doing things in short bursts, rather than one big stretch. So that may mean that three sessions of 20 minutes' focused attention are better than one long 60-minute slog. Try the 'short bursts' technique and see if it works for you.

Identify what sort of jobs or activities you can only spend a short time on. Are you easily bored or distracted or can you persevere on even the most difficult of tasks?

Compromise. Your job may not allow you to choose when you do particular tasks or activities, so you're going to have to be flexible and work out the best compromise possible.

Negotiate. If your best time of day is in the morning but you have other commitments that prevent you from using your optimal time for work that needs concentration and focus, if possible, negotiate with your manager or colleagues to free up some of your optimal time.

If you know the afternoon is your most productive time of day, don't allow yourself to be distracted or interrupted. Put the phone on answerphone and avoid looking at your emails!

FALLING ASLEEP

'Your future depends on your dreams. So go to sleep.' – Mesut Barazany

Sleep. It's where our brains travel to every night. It's the shift in consciousness that our bodies require every day.

If you're experiencing sleep problems, you're not alone: most of us have had trouble sleeping at one time or another. It's normal and usually temporary.

Often, you want to sleep but your brain keeps talking to itself. Your mind is in overdrive. Thoughts and worries seem to grow and loom larger at night. You need to switch off and sleep but there's nothing to distract you from thinking about what you did or didn't do or what you have yet to face. And in any case, night-time is not usually a practical time to do anything about whatever is worrying you.

There's no need to suffer in silence. Although you can't *make* yourself go to sleep, you can help sleep to occur by keeping yourself in the present.

In Practice

'A ruffled mind makes a restless pillow.' – Charlotte Brontë

Acknowledge and observe thoughts and feelings. Don't try to ignore, fight or control them. Instead, simply observe them without reacting or judging.

Let your thoughts go. Notice that when you don't try to control the thoughts they soon pass, like clouds moving across the sky. If you find yourself getting stuck on a particular thought, bring your attention back to your breathing. As you are being aware of your breathing, allow yourself to sink into the bed with each breath.

Write it down. If you can't fall asleep because of unwanted thoughts – concerns about money and work, relationship, family or health worries, for example – you may find it useful to write them down. This helps because you're externalizing your thoughts, getting them out of your head and down onto paper.

Open your eyes. If you're lying in bed and are unable to sleep, try keeping your eyes open. As they start to close, tell yourself to resist. Often, the more you try to stay awake, the sleepier you become.

 # BEING GENEROUS

'Give what you have. To someone, it may be better than you dare to think.'
– Henry Wadsworth Longfellow

Life is short. And we only get one shot at it. Those people who fully understand this recognize we have but a short time to make a contribution to the world, so they give to others and they share what they have.

Generosity can produce within you a sense that you are capable of making a difference in the world, that you are mindful of the needs of those around you and that you are making a contribution. It's the sincere desire to make others' lives easier and more pleasant by sharing what you have.

Opportunities for generosity are often around you. It doesn't have to be money or material things you give or share with others. Your time, energy, talents, experiences, knowledge and lessons learnt are all valuable. In fact, all these things are only as valuable as what you do with them, the extent to which you share them with others.

Generosity is unconditional. Just knowing you have made a difference forms the foundation for generosity. The world needs cheerful and generous givers. They improve society. They inspire us. They push us forward. You can be one of them.

In Practice

'You have not lived today until you have done something for someone who can never repay you.' – John Bunyan

Start with what you already have. Make a list of the things in your life you appreciate and for which you are grateful. Which of these things could you share with others? Think about the difference it could make to someone. Who would appreciate it too?

Double it. If you've never given away money, start by giving away a small amount. Then double it. Buy or cook someone a meal. Then invite some others. Leave a tip. Then double it. Whatever you do or give, go the extra mile.

Give from the heart. Give time, money or effort to something you believe in – something that's important to you. Is it the environment, poverty or a religion? Maybe it's world peace, child nutrition or animal rights? What about education, civil rights or clean water? Identify what already moves you, find an organization around that cause and help them in their work.

Then give something to a cause you have no interest or connection with but for which you recognize help and support is needed.

Find a person you believe in. If you find you are more easily motivated and shaped by the people in your life than organizations/causes, give something to that person instead.

Raise your awareness. Who do you know that's generous? Spend time with them and learn from them.

Live with less. Let go. Give things away instead of selling them.

FOCUSING YOUR MULTI-TASKING

'The only reason for time is so that everything doesn't happen at once.'
– Albert Einstein

You probably know someone who is good at multi-tasking. But are they really doing several things at once? Look closely and you may see that what they're actually doing is rapid task *switching*: rather than doing several things at once, they are doing several things, one thing at a time, but in quick succession.

With this sort of focused multi-tasking the brain is like a hotel room: one person occupies it and then moves out. Then another person moves in to occupy it. They are not both there at the same time.

If, like many of us, you find it difficult to multi-task, it's probably because you really are trying to do two things at once: surfing the Web while talking on the phone, writing while trying to follow a movie or composing an email while listening to the radio and eating a piece of toast.

Or, it may be that instead of focusing your attention exclusively on one task your mind is distracted thinking about the next task.

Your concentration isn't fully sustained on any of the tasks you juggle, so you end up using only a slice of your brain for each task.

To multi-task successfully, you need to do it mindfully. You need to do one thing at a time and focus on it completely. Then you move on to the next task or activity.

In Practice

'The successful man is the average man, focused.' – Unknown

Get better at task switching. Know what, exactly, you're going to be doing. Be clear about what tasks you are going to work on. Then decide how much time to give each task your full focus. Do it deliberately and completely. Then move on to the next task on your list.

Focus on one thing at a time. If you start thinking about other tasks, pause, breathe and pull yourself back.

Pair up compatible tasks. Although it's not possible to do several things at once, the exception is with compatible tasks. Reading at the same time as listening to someone talk is very difficult: they are too similar for your brain to manage both at once. However, doing a physical task (such as constructing or mending) with a mental task (such as listening to music or someone talking) is much more doable.

See if you work best by following one completed task with a similar related task, or if it helps to alternate completely different tasks. When you switch to a new task, your brain has to adjust. You may find that you can make this transition more easily if the tasks are related. You may, though, need a change in the nature of each task.

For example, you may or may not want to follow one meeting with another. You may want to follow a meeting with some time spent at your computer. Or you may need to take a short break before moving on to another task.

TUNING INTO YOUR INTUITION

'Trust yourself. You know more than you think you do.' – Benjamin Spock

Intuition is that keen and quick insight, that immediate knowing that tells you something is or isn't 'right'.

If you've ever had a moment where you felt as though something wasn't right – when things didn't seem to add up – then you've experienced intuition, an immediate knowing. Conversely, you could've experienced situations where everything *did* add up and seem to come together to tell you to take action straight away. That's also your intuition.

Tuning in to your intuition simply means being aware of the information your senses are communicating to you: what your ears, eyes, nose, sense of taste, sense of touch and the physical sensations are telling you.

Everyone has intuition. It bridges the gap between the conscious and non-conscious parts of your mind, between instinct and reason.

Intuitive messages are often keen and quick, which makes them easy to miss. So often, intuitive messages are drowned out by all the other internal and external noise and activity that is going on in and around you.

This is where mindfulness can help. The key to increasing your intuitive awareness is to be present. Intuition lives in the present. Mindfulness can help you filter out mental chatter and external noise, activity and distractions.

In Practice

'Your intuition knows what to do. The trick is to get your head to shut up so that you can hear.' – Louise Smith

Practise developing your intuition. Take a couple of minutes to be still and be present in a range of situations at home, on your way to work, at work, in a café, in the dentist's waiting room and so on. Breathe normally. What do you see or hear, smell, taste and feel?

Be aware of your thoughts. Notice physical sensations. Notice the temperature of the air as it flows through your nostrils. Notice the different smells in the air. What can you hear? Let the sounds you hear anchor you to the present moment.

Go outside. Changing your environment can help your senses get used to retuning. Observe the way the world is moving around you, the changing light, sights, sounds and smells.

Notice what's normal and what's new in familiar situations. Notice smells, sounds and sights; then, when you notice things being out of place or unusual, you will recognize your intuition communicating with you.

Tune in to your intuition. Learn to trust your instincts. If something doesn't feel right, focus. Don't allow anything else to divert your attention.

Listen to your body. In any one situation an inkling or flash of inner sense may be felt as a tightness in your chest, a lump in your throat, lightness in your head, a voice or a sensation, even a taste.

Be alert for a combination of signals. It may be a glimpse of something happening, a brief passing look from someone else and a momentary sound. When all the information your senses are receiving does add up, your intuition is coming through loud and clear

Other times, a single signal will be so strong you need no further signal – act now!

ASSERTING YOURSELF AND SAYING NO

'Assertiveness is not what you do; it's who you are!' – Cal Le Mon

Your manager asks you to take on a new project but you're not sure if you have the right skills and experience to do the work on your own and are worried about the consequences of saying no. A friend asks you to go to the cinema but you're too tired. Your brother asks you to have his children for a long weekend but you dread the thought and yet don't want to let him down.

Are there similar situations when you want to say no – to refuse assertively – but find yourself holding back because you aren't sure how to handle it?

Being assertive is an honest and appropriate expression of your feelings, opinions and needs. When you are assertive, you are able to let other people know, clearly and honestly, what you do and do not want, what you will or will not accept. You are open to other people's views even though they may be different from your own.

Assertiveness starts with being mindful. In any one situation or interaction with other people, you need to be aware of and acknowledge how you currently feel and what you do and don't want.

You need to be open and receptive to what other people think and feel so that when it's appropriate you can meet them halfway.

In Practice

'To know oneself, one should assert oneself.' – Albert Camus

Tune in to your mind. Start by noticing how you *feel* about the situation. Irritated? Ignored? Worried? Anxious? Rather than let your feelings take over the situation, let your feelings *inform* the situation. Acknowledging how you feel about a particular situation can help you clarify what you do or don't want.

Take your time. If you're not sure how you feel, simply tell the other person you're not sure and need time to think about it. Tell the other person when you will get back to them. And make sure you do get back to them.

Be clear and direct. Say what exactly it is you will or will not do. No waffling – that will only confuse the other person. Simply say, 'I'm sorry but I don't want to/can't do...'

Don't give lots of excuses. You only need one valid reason why you can't or won't do something.

Acknowledge what the other person says and feels. Once you have said what you do or do not want, you *must* stop and listen to the other person's response.

Accept the response but stand your ground. Calmly respond to the other person in a way that will both acknowledge what they've said and confirm you are standing firm.

Or, negotiate and cooperate. Settle by saying what you are prepared to do instead. For example, you'll take on the new project if you can have some help. You'll go to the cinema, but at the weekend, not this evening.

ACCEPTING THIS IS WHAT IT IS

'Of course there is no formula for success except, perhaps, an uncondi-
tional acceptance of life and what it brings.' – Arthur Rubinstein

Acceptance means understanding that things *are* (or *are not*) happening.

Mindfulness involves accepting what's happened and what's happening right now. It involves feeling whatever you feel without trying to resist or control those feelings or whatever is happening.

This doesn't mean you have to resign yourself to something, to give in. It means understanding that, at this moment, something is what it is.

Of course, life brings problems and difficulties and it's not easy to manage when you're suffering and wishing those things had never happened. But accepting what has happened means recognizing you cannot change what has *already* happened.

What could be more futile than resisting what already is? This doesn't mean you can't do anything about what's happening now, but before you do, you need to accept what has brought you to this point, to this present moment.

Once you accept something, rather than react to it (i.e. take impulsive, opposing action) you can respond to it (i.e. act thoughtfully and more favourably).

Acceptance brings a state of calm where you can rest without necessarily needing things to be different.

Acceptance happens in the moment.

In Practice

'Mindfulness is simply being aware of what is happening right now without wishing it were different; enjoying the pleasant without holding on when it changes (which it will); being with the unpleasant without fearing it will always be this way (which it won't).' – James Baraz

Think of something you find difficult to accept. Acknowledge what has happened. In your head or out loud describe what has happened. Allow yourself to feel angry, upset or disappointed about what has happened.

When you're ready, let go and move on to acceptance. Recognize that something has happened and you cannot change that.

Start out by accepting small things, such as missing the bus or train, or losing a pen or lighter, something that's not too important.

The ability to let go of small things in everyday life makes for acceptance, contentment and ease. Also, you will then be better placed to manage a missed opportunity, a sudden change in plans or serious loss.

Don't waste too much time, thought and energy being angry or upset. Use it more wisely.

You could complain for a long time about missing the train, losing your phone or feeling ill, but as long as you do, you can't do anything about it. You're stuck in what happened instead of moving forward into what you can do now.

Ask yourself, 'What can I do to solve the problem?' And if you can't solve it, where can you focus your energy more productively? 'What aspects of the situation do I have any control over?'

You can choose to focus on either what went wrong or what you can now do that's right. What would you choose?

OVERCOMING CRAVINGS

'Cravings and false hunger aren't the same as giving your body the fuel it needs.' – Deepak Chopra

Often, a food craving is strong enough to pick you up and carry you straight to the fridge or local shop.

Of course, an occasional craving is a pleasure to indulge, but if you find yourself regularly struggling to fight food cravings and would like to overcome them, mindfulness can help you break free from even the strongest cravings.

It helps to understand the nature of cravings. When you crave something, your attention has become fixated. Your attention becomes focused and fixed on the packet of crisps, chocolate or carrot cake etc. that you want. You can think of nothing else and a compelling momentum develops, a combination of thinking about that packet of crisps, chocolate or carrot cake and having a physical sensation.

With cravings, you focus on the desirable qualities of what you want, while ignoring the downside, the undesirable aspects or consequences of having given in to the craving.

By using conscious awareness to break your fixation you can separate wanting from getting. The present moment is always changing. Thoughts move in and out of your head. Sensations come and go. Cravings are no different. They do not last forever. Urges always pass eventually, whether or not you give in to them. Mindfulness can help.

In Practice

'There is no end of craving. Hence contentment alone is the best way to happiness. Therefore acquire contentment.' – Swami Sivananda

Acknowledge the craving. Recognize it as an urge, without trying to change it or get rid of it. Be aware of thoughts going through your mind and what the urge physically feels like. You can even name it in your head: 'Look at that, an urge to eat a bar of chocolate.'

Loosen the fixation. Remind yourself of your good intentions. This helps to keep you focused on what matters most and can get you through the moments when your impulses try to take over.

Breathe. Breathe mindfully. Focus on your breathing and you can put some space between your impulses and your actions by taking two minutes to engage in some mindful breathing.

Surf the urge. If you feel something pulling you away from your good intentions, 'surf the urge'. Imagine the urge as a wave in the ocean. It will build in intensity, but soon break and dissolve. Imagine yourself riding the wave, not fighting it but also not giving in to it. Know that cravings aren't permanent: they come and then they go. Just like the waves.

Distract your mind. Deliberately bring your attention to something that will help to divert your mind – something you know will engage you. Phone a friend for a chat, watch a film or read a book. Do something physical – go for a brisk walk, wash up, vacuum, sweep the path.

Be patient and kind to yourself. It's not easy to surf an urge, but each time you use mindful techniques, you weaken the craving.

PROBLEM SOLVING
WITH CREATIVE
THINKING

'Imagination will often carry us to worlds that never were. But without it we go nowhere.' – Carl Sagan

So often, problems, obstacles and difficulties at work are dealt with in the same old ways using the same methods and procedures.

It's easy to get stuck in habitual thought patterns, basing new ideas on what has or hasn't worked in the past. It can be hard to think outside these patterns and thinking ruts. But sticking to the usual ways of thinking can limit your creativity and options.

While mindfulness is about focusing on the present moment, there *is* an important place for mind wandering.

Sure, mind wandering can be unhelpful when thoughts wander to events and possibilities that are not related to what you're meant to be focusing on. *Mindful* mind wandering, on the other hand, is deliberate, purposeful and task related. In fact, it's completely necessary for imaginative, creative thinking.

Creative thinking enables you to transcend fixed ideas, rules and ways of doing things and instead create meaningful new ways, ideas and methods for doing things.

Mind wandering for creative problem solving can give you a new perspective and help you to come up with original, unconventional and innovative ideas.

Mindful mind wandering and creative thinking take a beginner's mind approach: you put aside beliefs and conclusions about what has and hasn't worked in the past and open up to new possibilities.

In Practice

'Creativity can be described as letting go of certainties.' – Gail Sheehy

Use a beginner's mind approach. To help you get into this mindset, instead of thinking what has and hasn't worked before, ask yourself what you would do if you didn't have any constraints in terms of money, time, resources or the people involved. Then what could be done? What options would you have? What would you choose to do?

Let your mind wander further. Imagine what ideas another individual, group or organization could come up with. For example, 'What would José Mourinho do? What would Beyoncé do? What would Primark or John Lewis do? What would someone you dislike intensely do?' Thinking in this way may seem a bit off the wall. The important thing at this stage is simply to imagine all sorts of possibilities and challenge assumptions about what is and isn't possible.

Be non-judgemental. Don't worry about only writing down the 'good' ideas and dropping 'bad' or 'ridiculous' ideas. Just capture as many new ideas as you can. Once you've come up with a range of ideas, options and possible solutions, you will find that one or two ideas can be developed into original, creative options and solutions to a situation.

Practise creative thinking. To get into the right frame of mind for creative mind wandering, think of 12 different uses for a house brick. For example, one use for a brick is as a doorstop. What else can you think of? Check your ideas by typing '12 uses for a brick' into a search engine and see what other ideas there are.

LETTING GO OF WORRY AND ANXIETY

'Worrying is using your imagination to create something you don't want.'
– Abraham Hicks

It only takes one event to turn out badly to 'prove' that things go wrong, and that you were 'right' to worry.

Certainly, worrying can be helpful when it spurs you to take action and solve a problem. But worrying on its own doesn't improve a situation. Worrying will not help you think clearly or help you deal with a potential problem.

Worry drags you out of the present moment and into an unknown future, allowing unrelenting doubts, fears and negative possibilities to overwhelm your mind and paralyse you.

Mindfulness can put a stop to this spiral of unhelpful thoughts and help you focus on the present moment, rather than pre-living the future.

In Practice

'Don't worry about the future; or worry, but know that worrying is as effective as trying to solve an algebra equation by chewing bubble gum.'
– Mary Schmich

Acknowledge, accept and let go. Instead of trying to fight or suppress troubling thoughts and worries, simply allow them to come and go. Say to yourself, 'Here's the thought that I could fail my exam/I won't get the job/I won't know anyone at the party.'

Each time a worrying thought enters your mind, acknowledge it and let it pass. Here are some ways to view worries and troubling thoughts:

- As items on a conveyer belt.
- As train carriages passing on a track.
- As clouds floating off in the sky.
- As helium balloons floating away.
- As leaves floating by on a stream.

Empty your mind. Externalize your thoughts, fears and worries about events by writing them down or telling someone. It's a helpful way to empty your mind so that you are free to focus on the present.

Look for solutions. Focus on what you *can* change, rather than aspects of the situation that are beyond your control. Find one small step you can take *now*, in the present moment. Once you start doing something about the problem, you may feel less worried because you are thinking and acting in the present rather than projecting yourself into the future.

Focus on what's happening right now. Identify activities that you can turn to when you want to switch off from worrying, something that you can dip into for ten minutes or immerse yourself in for an hour, something that keeps you focused and engaged, that brings your complete attention to the present experience.

MAKING SMALL TALK

'I'm not good at small talk. I'll hide in a cupboard to avoid chitty chat.'
– Caitlin Moran

Do you dread meeting people for the first time, wondering what you're going to say? Have you ever lingered in your car, lurked in the loo or simply pretended you haven't seen an acquaintance just to avoid making small talk?

Small talk doesn't come easily to all of us. Often, the fear of coming across as fake, dull or stupid makes it difficult to initiate small talk, let alone *maintain* a conversation.

Maybe you think small talk is pointless and claim to only be interested in 'real' conversation. But then how do you get to the point of having a deeper conversation with someone in the first place?

Conversation is like climbing a ladder, with small talk serving as the first few rungs. Small talk creates connections of all kinds. It's one way that you can open doors to all sorts of people and possibilities. After all, plenty of friendships, relationships and work connections have started with a few remarks about the weather!

The key is to be, or at least appear, friendly and approachable. Your aim is not to impress. It's to show you are a relaxed and sociable person who is open to exchanging a few pleasantries.

You simply never know when someone you meet will take your life in a new direction!

In Practice

'From small beginnings come great things.' – Proverb

Be aware and notice. Some of the easiest conversations come from what you've observed – something about where you both are, something you've observed someone reading, listening to, wearing or who else you've seen them talking to.

Start with a compliment. A good way to initiate small talk is to tie a compliment and a question together: 'I was really impressed with how you handled that. How did you manage to stay so calm?'

Say something about yourself. Say something about what you're interested in and then ask their opinion. You could, for example, say something about a book, blog or website you've found interesting or a film you have recently seen, or something funny, useful or interesting you heard on the radio or TV. Your work, travel, news stories, celebrity gossip: everything is a source of information, ideas and experiences that can be discussed.

Say whatever comes to your mind. Aim to say something to which the other person can make a comment or pose a question that will keep the conversation going. If you feel like talking about the pizza you had for breakfast, do that. If you follow it up with a question, 'What's the weirdest thing you've had for breakfast?' you've opened up the conversation.

Practise. Get used to talking to people you don't know and get in the habit of starting a conversation. Strike up some small talk with someone who works at a shop, café, cinema or theatre. They're used to people making small talk.

Let go. Know when to stop and pull out. You can't connect with everyone, and some conversations simply refuse to take life! Making small talk involves knowing when it's time to let go.

MAKING BALANCED DECISIONS

'Do not plant your dreams in the field of indecision, where nothing ever grows but the weeds of "what-if."' – Dodinsky

Decisions, decisions, decisions. How do you make the right choice, know that what you choose will work out and, if it doesn't, that you won't regret having made a different decision?

The answer is you don't, can't and won't. You can never know for sure when you make a decision that it's going to pan out as you'd hope.

Whether it's deciding which course, job or career or simply choosing something on the menu, often, a decision requires both intuition and reasoning. Sometimes these differ: your heart is pulling you one way but your head is pulling you another. It worries about the pros and cons and the consequences of a 'wrong' decision.

But overthinking can lead to confusion or obscure what you instinctively feel is the right path to take.

On the other hand, if you go with your heart, you wonder whether you are being too impulsive and may miss out on a 'better' option.

Sometimes you are so stuck you make no decision. And yet making no decision is still a decision – you've made a decision not to do anything.

What to do? Mindfulness can help you make decisions in a way that balances your emotional reactions with your logical responses. It can help you to acknowledge and accept uncertainty, making a choice despite possible unknowns.

In Practice

'In the midst of the flurry – clarity.
In the midst of the storm – calm.
In the midst of divided interests – certainty.
In the roads – a certain choice.' – Mary Anne Radmacher

In any one situation where you are finding it difficult to make a decision:

- **Use your head.** Identify your values: what's important to you – and your aims? What are you hoping to achieve? Identifying your values and aims focuses your mind and narrows your choices so that you pay attention to relevant factors and not irrelevant ones.
- **Listen to your heart.** When your heart – your intuition – tells you that a particular path or choice is the right one, that's because your decision is in line with your aims and values. The 'This is it!' feeling never feels conflicted or forced. Instead, it feels right.
- **Let go of fear.** Accept uncertainty. Make a choice despite possible unknowns. Know there is no 'right' or 'wrong' decision. Instead, ask yourself, 'What's the worst that can happen? How might I deal with that?' Know that if things don't work out, if and when that time comes, you can act on it then.
- **Start again with a beginner's mind.** Whether you choose this queue or that queue – this job or career or that job or career, if it didn't work out, you can think about what you learnt from that situation. What did you learn that you could use to inform a similar decision next time?

When you have to make a quick decision, toss a coin. Why? Because often when the coin is in the air, in that moment, you will know what you are hoping for!

PUTTING JEALOUSY
BEHIND YOU

'It is not love that is blind, but jealousy.' – Lawrence Durrell

There's always someone you know who has a great lifestyle, relationship, house or job. There are always others with more money, lots of friends and a nicer family. Someone who is younger, better dressed and cleverer. In fact, there's always someone somewhere in a seemingly better position than you.

A touch of jealousy can be useful. It can push you – even inspire you – to improve your situation and to achieve more.

However, when jealousy overwhelms you it has the opposite effect, since your narrow, closed mind keeps out any possibility of moving forward in a positive way. You're stuck. Stuck in your jealousy.

When jealousy gets a grip on you, you compare your situation with theirs and find yours wanting.

Maybe someone else's position makes you feel threatened, or not good enough, unsure of yourself and your abilities or achievements. Maybe you feel that their strengths highlight your weaknesses. Perhaps you simply resent them for 'making' you feel jealous – trapped in a downward spiral of bitterness and anger.

Jealousy can make you lose touch with who you are. You create a false illusion of yourself based on and comparing yourself with someone else, and who they are and what they have.

You can only see what they have and what you have not.

Instead of fixating on what you don't have, mindfulness encourages you to focus and engage with what you *do* have and to work on getting what you want.

In Practice

'Don't waste your time on jealousy; sometimes you're ahead, sometimes you're behind ... the race is long, and in the end, it's only with yourself.'
– Mary Schmich

Acknowledge your jealousy. The next time you catch yourself resenting what someone else has and feeling a sense of hurt combined with entitlement, recognize it for what it is: jealousy. Acknowledge it by simply saying to yourself, 'This is jealousy.'

Observe it. You can do this quite literally: write down how you feel and then look at and read what you've written.

Sit with it. Use mindful breathing techniques to calm your mind and the intensity of the emotion.

Let it pass. Let it go. Tell yourself that you don't need this emotion and you're relinquishing it.

Learn from it. What is it that someone else has that you want? Use a beginner's mind. Focus on starting over and achieving what it is you want to achieve. Rather than get stuck in your jealousy – 'Why have they got it? I want what they've got!' – change your focus. Focus on how you can work towards what you want.

Accept it. If it's not possible to have what the other person has, accept it. Stop comparing yourself. Instead, ground yourself and focus on what you *do* have and what you *can* achieve.

SPENDING TIME WITH POSITIVE PEOPLE

'Surround yourself only with people who are going to lift you higher.' –
Oprah Winfrey

It's not difficult to spot positive people. Positive people are people you feel good being around. They're people you can be yourself with.

A positive person could be the person who supports you when you're down and is fun when you're up. They could be someone who provides wisdom and advice when you're lost and confused, someone who sees your strengths even when you don't.

A positive person could be someone you know who is open-minded, kind, compassionate and generous. They could be someone you know who is courageous about following their dreams; he or she inspires you.

Imagine a fish that grows in proportion to its environment. If you keep it in a pail of water, it only grows a couple of inches. But if you place it in a lake, it can grow up to two feet. Are you like a fish that has been kept in a pail?

When you spend time with positive people, the boundaries of what is possible expand. Which, in turn, gives you the ability to consider new ideas and new possibilities.

You become like the company you keep. So choose carefully.

In Practice

'Good people bring out the good in people.' – Unknown

Who in your life fits the descriptions on this list?

- Someone who makes me feel good about myself.
- Someone I can totally be myself with.
- Someone who listens to what I've got to say.
- Someone I can talk to if I am worried.
- Someone who makes me laugh.
- Someone who inspires me.
- Someone who introduces me to new ideas, interests or new people.

You may have a different person or a number of people for each situation. Or the same one or two people may feature on the list. The people on your list do not just have to be friends or family; they could be colleagues or neighbours.

Adopt a beginner's mind and think creatively. The person who makes you laugh could be a comedian on the TV. The person who you can turn to when you're worried may be someone in a support group, a financial adviser or your GP. The person who inspires you could be someone you have read about who has overcome adversity.

Read about positive people – ordinary people or famous people – who inspire you. But don't just read about positive people. Search them out. Search out people who have the same interests as you.

Look on the Internet to find people who can introduce you to new ideas and interests. Join a class or a special interest group with like-minded people to develop an interest (singing, tennis, walking, local history, for example) or promote a cause (raising money for cancer research, renovating a local building, for example).

HOLDING BACK FROM OVEREATING

'My doctor told me I had to stop throwing intimate dinners for four unless there are three other people.' – Orson Welles

These days, food is more available, more affordable, more plentiful and more wide ranging than ever before.

It's easy to overeat, to eat more than you need. Some people have a sweet tooth; others prefer savoury. Some pile up their plates; others continually nibble.

Perhaps you eat even when you're not hungry and often you continue eating even after you're full, mindless of the process of eating and the sensation of being full. You can eat an entire meal, a whole sandwich or cake and not taste more than a bite or two. This is because your mind and mouth weren't present, weren't tasting or enjoying, as you ate.

If you do give it any thought, maybe you think you *should* or *must* finish what's on your or even someone else's plate. Otherwise, the food will be wasted.

How and what you eat has a lot to do with habit, repeating past triggers, thoughts and feelings about food and eating again and again. Mindfulness increases your awareness of these patterns without judgement and creates space between mindless eating and mindful eating.

In Practice

'Eating is a natural way to feel happy. Overeating isn't.' – Deepak Chopra

Think before you eat. Take a moment to ask yourself how hungry you are on a scale of 1 to 10, and how that hunger matches up with what you have in front of you. Remember, you don't *have* to clear your plate.

Pay attention. Don't eat in front of the TV or computer, while standing at the kitchen counter or talking on the phone. This can lead to losing track of how much you've consumed. Remind yourself of the Zen proverb: 'When walking, walk. When eating, eat.'

Slow down. Apparently, it can take your body up to 20 minutes to register the fact that you're full and during that time you may be continuing to eat. Slow down. Put your fork down every few mouthfuls. Check how you're feeling. 'Am I still hungry, or am I full?'

Use smaller plates. Using a nine-inch plate instead of a 12-inch plate means smaller portions. Apparently, studies have shown food consumption is 22 per cent lower when eating from a smaller plate.

Take notice. If you go out to eat, notice how much you're eating. You don't have to eat all of the chips: you can eat just a handful. Think about what you really love to eat, and save the calories for those foods. Does that cheese on the burger really make it for you? If not, that's about a hundred calories. Gravy, salad dressing, butter... you have control of how much you really need or want on there.

BEING
NON-JUDGEMENTAL

'When you judge another, you don't define them, you define yourself.'
– Wayne W. Dyer

Being non-judgemental means that rather than evaluate what is happening, rather than see something as 'good' or 'bad', 'right' or 'wrong', you just experience or observe it.

You don't need to give any meaning to events, your thoughts, feelings and actions or other people's actions. You are simply looking at things in an objective way as opposed to having an opinion about them.

In fact, it's only when you give thoughts to experiences and events that they have any meaning.

In his book *Origin of the Species*, Charles Darwin doesn't describe anything – any plant or animal – as 'beautiful', 'ugly', 'frightening' or 'timid'. He simply categorizes things according to a common descent.

Left to itself, your mind will often judge things as good or bad, right or wrong, fair or unfair, important or unimportant, urgent or non-urgent and so on. This happens so fast that your experiences are coloured almost as soon as they occur.

Mindfulness is about being aware of that and taking a fresh perspective. It involves noticing your experience as it is and not as your mind judges it. This approach can then open you to the possibility of thinking about things in a different way.

In Practice

'Do not judge and you will never be mistaken.'
– Jean-Jacques Rousseau

Be aware of when your mind is judging something. You may be surprised how often you judge something as pleasant or unpleasant throughout the day. Your senses check and label experiences: seeing, hearing, tasting, smelling, touching and thinking.

Try writing down all the judging, evaluating, appraising and so on that goes on in your mind during the course of a few hours. Write down all the things that you did, that happened, that other people did. Then remember what thoughts you attached to those actions. Be aware of how your mind judges everything and actively separates everything into good and bad and right and wrong.

Next, instead of writing about what *has* happened, write about what *is* happening. Write about your experience in the here and now. Simply *describe* what you can see, hear, feel or smell.

Avoid using evaluative words – words that measure or compare what you see, taste, smell etc. Instead, just describe... that's being non-judgemental.

DOING WORK THAT MATCHES YOUR VALUES

'Don't worry about what the world needs. Ask what makes you come alive and do that. Because what the world needs is people who have come alive.'
– Howard Thurman

Not caring about your work, that there's little point to it, feeling that you're not fulfilling your potential but not knowing what else you can do can leave you feeling bored, frustrated and even depressed.

When you do enjoy your work then you're doing something that matches your interests, strengths and values. Your work reflects the real you, the person you really are right now. You're present, focused and engaged in what you're doing and not wishing you were somewhere else in a different job.

In order to take steps towards doing the work *you* want to do, it's helpful to identify what your values are. Throughout your life you acquire a set of values: beliefs, ideas and qualities that are important to you. For example, you may believe that you should always be honest or that you must always be loyal and committed. Whatever you believe, your values are a central part of who you are and who you want to be.

When what you do does not align with your values, things feel wrong. But when the things that you do match your values, you feel confident that you are doing the right thing. You'll also be able to take advantage of opportunities when they present themselves. It's not about becoming a different person: it's about becoming more of the real you.

In Practice

'Only the truth of who you are, if realized, will set you free.' – Eckhart Tolle

Know what's important to you. What do you value? To help you get started, consider these personal values:

Compassion, adventure, independence, inclusivity, excitement, honesty, reliability, peace, risk, creativity, acceptance, fun, belonging, cooperation, certainty.

To think more about this, type the words 'list of values' into a search engine for a long list of values that will help you decide which values are important to you.

Next, focus on specific *work* values, the things that are important to you in the work you do. Here are examples of work values: helping others, prestige and status, good job security, teamwork, working on my own, being appreciated, high pay, leadership and influence, variety, challenge, creativity, routine and procedure.

Type 'work values' into a search engine for a more comprehensive list of values that will help you decide which work values are important to you.

If your job, your work or your career does not reflect your values, think about the type of work or career that would reflect your values.

Be patient. Keep in mind that your values are guiding principles: they will need to be flexible and you may have to compromise for a time, depending on what other commitments you have in your life.

If you cannot meet your values in your current job, find ways to meet them in other areas of your life. If, for example, your office-based job doesn't align with your values of risk, adventure and challenge, what leisure activities could you do that would meet those values?

BUILDING YOUR COURAGE

'Courage is being scared to death, but saddling up anyway.' – John Wayne

Courage. Now there's an old-fashioned word. In medieval times, courage, along with prudence, justice and temperance, was considered one of the four cardinal virtues. It brings to mind fierce determination, or fighting against all odds.

The word 'courage' comes from the French word *coeur*, which means 'heart'. Courage is a state of the heart. It's the ability to do what feels right, even if it scares you.

Courage is the quality of mind or spirit that enables you to face difficulty despite your fear and concerns. Courage gives you the ability to do something that frightens you. It is strength in the face of pain, hostility or intimidation.

Whether it's leaving your job or a relationship, moving to a new town, standing up for yourself or someone else, courage is what makes you brave and helps you take action.

Each day there may be situations where you need to make a courageous choice. You may need courage to present a new idea at work, to stand up for yourself or to make a decision that others won't like.

Courage often requires you to act as if you're confident, whatever you actually feel. Confidence and courage come through acting as if you are unafraid, even when you are.

In Practice

'I learned that courage was not the absence of fear, but the triumph over it. The brave man is not he who does not feel afraid, but he who conquers that fear.' – Nelson Mandela

Build your courage. Do one thing every day that scares you and feel your courage grow.

Here're some ideas:

- **Start something new.** It takes courage to learn something new. Take a new exercise class, even though you don't know the moves.
- **Go somewhere you've never been before.** Take a different way to and from work. Go to a different restaurant from the ones you usually choose. Go somewhere new. If you usually go with other people, go on your own.
- **Say what's in your heart.** Speak up when you'd usually keep quiet.
- **Shout.** On a deserted beach, in your car or into a pillow. The shout that comes from within can be a source of energy and courage.

Tap in to your courage. Think of a situation when you felt afraid, yet faced your fear and took action. What helped? What did other people do or say that helped give you courage? What did you think or feel? Experience that courage in this moment, right now: feel the strength of courage.

Focus. Courage comes from being motivated by a clear goal or sense of duty. Focusing on why you're doing something and what you want to achieve, keeping that in your mind, stops you from allowing feelings of doubt, uncertainty and fear to creep in.

Breathe in to your heart. Remember, courage means 'heart'. Keep yourself calm and focused by doing a heart-centred breath. Place your hand on your heart and visualize breathing in and out of that heart space.

BEING PERSUASIVE

'My most brilliant achievement was my ability to persuade my wife to marry me.' – *Winston Churchill*

Most of us find ourselves having to persuade someone at some point. Maybe you've wanted to persuade a colleague to do a piece of work with you or you've wanted to persuade your manager to take on your brilliant idea. Perhaps you've tried to persuade your teenager to join in with a family event or your partner to agree to a holiday somewhere.

Persuasion is not about trying to *make* someone do something or to argue that your idea or way of doing something is best. That would probably put most people on the defensive.

Persuasion requires the mindful qualities of engagement, acknowledgement and patience. In order to convince someone to do what you want, you will need to explain what it is you want them to do and what they may stand to gain. Appeal to reason and feelings. You have to be prepared to negotiate and compromise with the person you're hoping to persuade.

In Practice

Be patient. It's not just what you say, it's *when* you say it. If possible, wait for a time when the other person is going to be most present, receptive and open to considering your proposal.

Engage. Ask yourself what you already know about the other person that could help you to engage him or her. What could catch their interest? Are you relying on past knowledge of the other person? Rather than relying on the usual ways of persuading and motivating others, try a new approach. Ask them what their interests and goals are.

Listen. One of the best ways to persuade people is with your ears, by listening to them. Listen to the other person's objections. Acknowledge and address those objections. People are far more willing to cooperate if they feel acknowledged and understood.

Be ready to find the easiest path to yes. Negotiate and compromise. Explain what you're ready to do or concede.

Be patient and wait. Urgency and immediacy are often the enemies of persuasion. People are best brought on board in their own time. Make your suggestion and leave them to think about it.

Let go. Know when to accept that the other person is not going to come round to your way of thinking. Let it go. Give up trying to persuade and, instead, formulate a plan B.

COMMUTING: TAKING IT IN YOUR STRIDE

'Travelling. It leaves you speechless. Then turns you into a storyteller.'
– Ibn Battuta

Like any journey, journeys to and from work are times of transition. And in times of transition, your mind is likely to be either projecting into the future (you are, after all, going somewhere) or dwelling on what you've just left behind.

Maybe you see your daily commute as a time between other obligations, when what you have left at work has stayed at work and you haven't yet become immersed in home activities. Your commute may be the one part of the day when you can disconnect, a perfect time to spend time listening to music, podcasts and audiobooks.

Or perhaps you see it as a stressful waste of your time, particularly when unexpected delays, interruptions and cancellations occur due to weather, 'technical difficulties', strikes or other reasons beyond your control.

The lack of information and uncertainty make you anxious, which makes the wait seem longer. You're powerless. It feels unfair and you start getting wound up – even angry. And yet, delays and cancellations are inevitable – this is the reality of travel.

How to remain calm, patient and flexible so that you can take commuting and any delays in your stride? A mindful approach can help you to keep your cool until you get on your way again.

Reframing the way you view the trip can turn your commute from a daily source of stress into a peaceful time to yourself between the demands of work and home.

In Practice

'Wherever you go, go with all your heart.' – Confucius

If you're driving, drive mindfully. Feel the movement of the steering wheel in your hands. Feel your feet on the pedals. Notice the sound as you change gear. Check the mirrors and notice details about the road ahead to stay involved in the world around you.

Leave plenty of time. That way, if you are delayed, you can minimize the stress of running late. And if you end up arriving early, you can spend the extra time doing something mindful.

Delays are inevitable. You know that. So plan for them. On a train or bus, read or listen to music. Take a short break in between chapters or tracks to look out the window and notice the passing scene. Notice the rhythm and gentle sway of the train.

If you get caught up in a delay, once you have accepted that the delay *has* happened and there's nothing you can do to change that, you can focus on what you *are* able to control. You can, for example, phone ahead and let others know you'll be late. Maybe you could ask for someone to pick you up at the other end when you arrive or plan to get a taxi for the last part of your journey.

Remind yourself that getting stressed or anxious won't change things for the better. Spend your time and effort on staying calm. Breathe. On a delayed, crowded bus or train, this can give you a sense of space. Be patient. Things will unfold in their own time. Remind yourself that this too will pass.

TAKING CONTROL OF ANGER

'Anger is an acid which can do more harm to the vessel in which it is stored than to anything on which it is poured.' – Mark Twain

You're angry. The whole world narrows down. Your heart races. Your breathing is fast and shallow. Your muscles are tense.

It's not wrong to feel angry. Anger is a normal emotion, a natural response to feeling wronged, offended, threatened or attacked in some way.

The problem is it's easy to become irrational and illogical when you're angry because the anger has overwhelmed and shut down your rational mind. So, whatever your anger is about, it can cause you to do things you will regret.

Keeping calm is not easy, but in order to think straight you need to get a grip. It's just like putting your own oxygen mask on in a damaged aeroplane before helping those around you. If you pass out, you can't help anyone. And, if when you're angry, you lose control, you are no good to yourself or anyone else. If you are cool, calm and collected, on the other hand, you will be ready and able to think clearly and respond appropriately.

So, you need to reduce the possibility of losing control and increase your ability to think more clearly. A mindful response can occur in the same time as an angry reaction, but the outcome will be totally different.

Using mindful techniques won't mean you never get angry, but they are a good start to slowing everything down and giving you a chance to think more clearly and then respond more appropriately.

In Practice

'If you are patient in a moment of anger, you will escape one hundred days of sorrow.' – Chinese proverb

Be aware of your own physical warning signs of anger.

You may feel:

- Your heart rate and breathing increase.
- Your jaw clenching.
- Your body becoming tense.
- Your voice becoming louder and sharper.

Stop for a few moments and simply breathe. Focus on your breathing.

Engage your mind. Divert it with something that won't take too much effort. Here're some ideas:

- Recite the alphabet backwards in your head.
- Count backwards in odd numbers, from 59: 59, 57, 55, 53 and so on.
- Visualize what you did yesterday from when you woke up until you went to bed.
- Recite a poem or the words of a song in your head.
- Create a mindful space for your anger. It *will* pass.
- Let out the need to lash out by hitting a cushion and/or crying, shouting, screaming or swearing where it will not alarm anyone.
- Go for a walk, run or cycle or do any other form of exercise that you enjoy.
- Sing out loud to fast, loud music. This can help you release some of the energy that comes with anger.
- Or, to help change your mood and calm down, listen to soothing music.
- Phone a friend. Tell them what happened and how angry you are.

Once you've mindfully managed your anger, you can think straight and decide what to do next. Don't think for so long, though, that your anger builds back up again!

DEALING WITH RUDENESS

'To penetrate the hardest armour, use the softest touch.' – Haven Trevino

A few years ago, writer and teacher Arthur Rosenfeld was in a drive-thru queue at a Starbucks in Florida. The man in the car behind him was getting impatient and angry, leaning on his horn and shouting insults at both Arthur and the Starbucks workers.

'I'll show you what happens to rude and impatient people,' thought Arthur. But then he caught himself and noticed that his face was as twisted with anger and hate as the man's behind him.

In one moment Arthur had what he calls a 'change of consciousness': he chose to keep calm and change the negativity into something positive. Arthur paid for both his and the other man's order and then went on his way. When he got home, Arthur discovered that his actions had featured on NBC News. Within twenty-four hours, news of what he had done had spread around the world via the Internet and television.

No doubt, you too have met mean, rude people. You're going about your day when out of the blue someone pulls their car abruptly in front of you or they jump the queue. Perhaps they interrupt you repeatedly when you're talking or say or write something horrible to deliberately hurt your feelings.

Usually, when others are rude or hostile, we jump at the chance to assume the worst and defend or attack. How can you – like Arthur Rosenfeld – have a 'change of consciousness'? How do you reach inside and pull out kindness when it's the furthest thing from your mind?

In Practice

'Silence the angry man with love. Silence the ill-natured man with kindness. Silence the miser with generosity. Silence the liar with truth.'
– Buddha

Practise responding with kindness. Next time you read or listen (on the radio, TV or overheard in public) to someone else's opinion and it really annoys you, think about giving them the benefit of the doubt. Believe something good about someone, rather than something bad.

Suspend judgement. Assume the other person has had a difficult day and, unfortunately, is taking it out on you. Try to keep an overall positive impression of others, and keep their negative qualities in the larger context of their good *and* bad nature. With this perspective, you will be in a much better position to respond with positivity.

Next time someone is mean or rude to you in person, breathe. Count backwards, from seven. Be aware of how you react: notice that your body has tensed and your mind is attempting to assign meaning and blame.

Know when to let it go. If you can make an appropriate, kind gesture to the other person, go ahead. But if they reject it or if the person is someone you don't know, walk away. Maya Angelou once said, 'When someone shows you who they are, believe them the first time.' The last thing you want is to get yourself into trouble. People who are mean and rude are stressed out and can flip at any time. Do or say one wrong thing and you could end up in trouble.

UNDERSTANDING WHERE YOUR FOOD COMES FROM

'Tell me what you eat, I'll tell you who you are.' – *Jean Anthelme Brillat-Savarin*

Most of us are far removed from the source of our food. If we think about where our food comes from, we picture food shops and supermarkets, not farms. We interact with cashiers, not growers.

Of course, industrial farming has many benefits: innovation in farming and technology and participation in global trade, availability of different varieties of food. Yet it also has drawbacks. It can damage the environment, harm workers, undermine rural communities and compromise animal welfare. Industrial farming can disconnect us from the food we eat.

And yet, a hundred years ago it was normal practice to buy local food.

A mindful approach can encourage you to think about where the food you are eating has come from. Who grew it or raised it? How? Where did it come from? How did it get here? Chances are, you'll not only gain more appreciation for your food but also find your shopping habits changing in the process.

From planting a vegetable garden to visiting a farmers' market, the answer is hardly that simple, but it's a start – it's a mindful start.

In Practice

'That's the most interesting thing about food –that it's a process, not a product. Everything in the grocery store has had a fascinating life, but most people only see a moment in the cycle of each food.'
– Barbara Kingsolver

Visit a farm shop. There are now several thousand farm shops in the UK. Find one that's near where you live and start using it. Connect with people who actually raise the animals and grow the crops.

Raise your children's awareness. Help your children learn about where their food comes from. The British Nutrition Foundation's website http://www.foodafactoflife.org.uk has a useful range of activities for children and young people to explore how food grows, where their food comes from, how food is processed, what foods are in season and so on.

Learn to forage. Thought there was no such thing as a free lunch? Whether you live in the country or the city, Britain's edible wild plants, berries and nuts can provide exactly that.

Before you head out into the wilderness, do check whether the land you are foraging on is protected and whether it is public. Get permission if it isn't. Always follow the country code and don't overharvest: birds and animals depend on wild foods for their survival.

Take precautions and get some tips and advice from experienced foragers. This is essential. Visit a website such as http://www.tasteth-ewild.co.uk/ or Richard Maybey's book *Food for Free* to find out more and you could soon be enjoying the simple pleasures of wild garlic, nettles, elderflowers, wild fennel, wild plums and figs.

UNDERSTANDING THAT ALL THINGS COME AND GO

'Sunrise doesn't last all morning. A cloudburst doesn't last all day.' – George Harrison

Everything comes into and leaves this world as the result of a combination of causes and conditions. Your thoughts come and go. Rivers run fast then slowly. You are born then you pass away. Nothing is permanent and all eventually ends.

Mindfulness helps you to understand this. You can appreciate the good, the enjoyable and happy times. You will be more able to make the most of now, knowing it will not last.

You will also know that suffering, problems and difficulties will not last. One way or another, they will pass.

Mindfulness helps you to recognize the futility of hanging on or getting attached to thoughts, feelings, ideas, people and events. They will pass anyway.

In Practice

'The days come and go like muffled and veiled figures sent from a distant friendly party, but they say nothing and if we do not use the gifts they bring, they carry them silently away.' – Ralph Waldo Emerson

Look for examples of the impermanence of things – objects, experiences and feelings, the people in your life.

Close your eyes and listen to how sounds appear and disappear.

Pleasure does not last, so make the most of it now. The chocolate meditation is a good example of this.

1. Break off a square of chocolate and place it in your mouth and allow it to slowly melt into the warmth of your tongue.
2. Reflect on, and fully enjoy, the flavour and texture of the chocolate.
3. Notice how the taste and texture change from the time you first place the chocolate into your mouth to the time it is completely melted.

We've all suffered pain and loss. Think back to a difficult time. Then recall how that time was not permanent. Remind yourself of this when you are in the middle of a difficult, challenging experience. Remind yourself 'this too shall pass'.

SWITCHING OFF THE ENGINE OF YOUR MIND

'I like my new phone, my computer works just fine, my calculator is perfect, but Lord, I miss my mind!' – Unknown

Sometimes, it can feel like work is taking over your life. It's not just that you spend most of your day at work: even when you're not there, you're still thinking about it.

With constant access to the Internet, emails and texts, it's easy to stay plugged in all day when you're at work and when you're away from it. You can find yourself in a mode of permanent activity with little in the way of a rest or break from technology which puts you somewhere that you're not.

But just as you wouldn't leave the engine of your car running when it's parked outside, so you need to switch off the engine of your mind.

In fact, in 2013, the German employment ministry (following moves by companies such as Puma, Volkswagen and BMW) issued guidelines stating that workers were not expected to check email at weekends or in their free time, to prevent employees from burning out.

The guidelines – drawn up to protect workers' mental health – state that staff should not be penalized for switching off their mobiles or leaving their emails unanswered when they are not at work. Managers aren't allowed to call or email staff except in emergencies, to make sure staff 'disconnect' outside of working hours.

Your employer and technology aren't totally to blame, though. You need to take responsibility. You need to learn how to disengage, to separate work life and free time.

In Practice

'We're constantly bombarded with information, and the only solution is to switch off for a while.' – Danny Penman

Practise disconnecting. If you work on a computer most of the day, have times when you disconnect so you can focus on other things. Taking even short breaks from technology can help. Leave your desk at lunchtime and try leaving your phone at your desk.

Switch your electronics off a few hours before you go to bed. Unless your job specifically requires you to be on call 24/7, there's little that happens after 8 p.m. that can't wait until the morning.

Over the weekend, consider having an afternoon or even a full day to disconnect. Get used to being without your phone, tablet or laptop. Get some fresh air. Go hiking or cycling. Play a sport. Take a phone but turn it off. Concentrate on something else. Have a go at something creative, artistic or musical,

When it comes to holidays, try a new approach to dealing with that post-holiday email mountain. A standard out-of-office message usually says: 'I'm now away until ... and will deal with your email on my return.' Instead, leave this message. 'Many thanks for your mail. Unfortunately, I won't be able to read it, as I am away until ... and all my emails will be automatically deleted. Please email again after that date.'

Worry about missing out? Sure, that's a possibility. But take a proper break.

BUILDING UP YOUR WILLPOWER

'The first step to becoming it is to will it.' – Mother Teresa

Willpower is the power of choice, of actually doing what you've chosen to do – what you intend to do – even when you don't feel like it. Willpower is the inner determination that drives you forward. It enables you to keep focused and achieve your goals.

We've all had good intentions. Maybe you've promised yourself you're going to get up early and do some chores. Perhaps you intend to eat something healthy for lunch, fill in that job application this evening or go for a run at the weekend.

So what stops you? Why is willpower so difficult to maintain? According to several studies, we all have a limited amount of willpower and it is easily used up. When you have to exercise willpower and self-control in one situation, there is less willpower available to you for other situations, even if those situations are totally different from each other.

Spend an hour (reluctantly) writing a report or putting together a presentation, and even though you intended to write your Christmas cards or go for a run afterwards, your brain doesn't have enough energy left to motivate you. You've used up your willpower and fallen victim to 'can't power'.

The good news is that you can build up your willpower in a mindful way, by focusing on activities that require a small amount of willpower. Rather than think about things you need to motivate yourself for at some future point in the day, you use your motivation to do small things in the present.

In Practice

'Stop saying, "I wish", start saying, "I will."' – Unknown

Focus on doing just one small thing you don't feel like doing. Then, when you've completed it, be aware of how you feel now, in the present moment for having achieved it.

Here're some ideas to get you started.

- Make your bed every morning.
- Go for a ten-minute walk every lunchtime.
- Walk up the stairs, rather than take the lift.
- Get off the tube or bus one stop earlier or park your car ten minutes from your destination and walk the rest of the way.
- Do something for someone else – make them a cup of tea or coffee.

Set yourself up for success. You can really help yourself by putting things into place which will make it more likely you'll follow through with your good intentions. So start by doing one small thing – one small step – towards what you intend to do.

Focus on the benefits, not the difficulties. Instead of thinking about how hard something is, think about what you will get out of it. For example, rather than think about how you can't be bothered, focus on how good you'll feel when you're done.

Approach situations with a beginner's mind. Put aside your judgements and beliefs about what you can or can't do. If you don't do what you intended to do, don't give up. You can always start again. Tell yourself 'I can' and 'I will.'

PRACTISING COMPASSION

'My mission in life is not merely to survive, but to thrive and to do so with passion, some compassion, some humour and some style.' – Maya Angelou

Compassion is what you feel for a person – or animal – who has been struck by misfortune. It motivates you to do something to help. Compassion reflects the idea that everything is related to everything else. Compassion allows you to be aware of the connection you have with everyone and everything.

When you are centred on yourself and focused on your own concerns, it's difficult to have compassion for others, to look beyond yourself and notice other people who are struggling in some way.

Compassion is mindful. It requires you to actively look for – to be aware and notice – positive ways to reach out to help and support someone who is suffering or finding it difficult to cope.

As the Dalai Lama says, 'The true aim of the cultivation of compassion is to develop the courage to think of others and to do something for them.'

Although compassion expects no reward or recognition, doing something to benefit someone else can make you *and* the person you are helping feel good. This can create a bond between you. It can help you to develop empathy and bring a fresh perspective to your own life and circumstances.

In Practice

'If you want others to be happy, practise compassion. If you want to be happy, practise compassion.' – Dalai Lama

Raise your awareness. Be open to the difficulty, the struggle, the impact of events, the stress, sorrow and strain in others. Who in your life could benefit from compassion? Someone who is lonely, unwell, worried and anxious about something? Maybe a friend tells you about a loss, or you can see the hurt behind someone's angry face. Be open to compassion from time to time for people you don't know: a harassed-looking parent, a tired commuter. Moments of compassion come in the flow of life. Do something small each day to help: smile, offer a kind word or a supportive comment.

Remember when someone has shown you compassion. What did they do that helped? What wasn't so helpful?

What do you think the person to whom you are showing compassion may find helpful? Ask them. Ask if you can help. People often find it difficult to ask for help. They feel that they are inconveniencing the other person or being a burden. The next time you see someone who looks down or frustrated, offer to help them. Simply ask how you could help make a situation better.

If you have already thought of something you could do that may help, it may be appropriate to ask if they are okay with your helping out in that way.

MEETING DEADLINES

'I like deadlines. I like the whooshing sound they make as they go by.'
– Douglas Adams

Too much to do and too little time to do it all. Sometimes it can seem endless.

When you think about what you have to do and the deadlines you have to meet, it's easy to panic and think, 'I'm never going to be able to get this done in time!'

Working in a job that requires you to meet constant deadlines is demanding. Stress can overtake your mind and prevent you from thinking clearly and staying present.

You feel that everything is urgent, unending and unbeatable. It's not. In fact, some people thrive in this sort of environment. How come? Because they know some of the mindful ways to successfully work towards deadlines. They're completely focused. By planning and prioritizing they're able to create environments – both internal and external – that support the achievement of those tasks. You can learn to do this too.

There *is* light at the end of the tunnel.

In Practice

'Planning is bringing the future into the present so that you can do something about it now.' – Alan Lakein

Stop trying to get ahead of yourself. You'll be spinning from one thing to the next. Instead, prioritize. Work out what's really important, what tasks will contribute to meeting that deadline. Ditch the other tasks and do the rest in order of importance.

Focus. Decide what the single-most-important or pressing task is and what is the one thing you can do right now. Then do that *one* thing. Give it your full attention. Once that one thing is done, ask yourself the same question, and do another single step. Give that your full attention too. Be deliberate and purposeful, not rushed and random. Repeat as needed and give yourself short breaks along the way.

Plan the tasks – the steps you need to take – and think through how you will do them. How is this mindful? As Alan Lakein says, 'Planning is bringing the future into the present so that you can do something about it now.' It's easier to get straight on to the next step if you have already planned what you are going to do and how you are going to do it. It allows you to maintain a steady pace and maintain the pace when the deadline comes closer. Tell yourself, 'I have a plan. I can manage this.'

Remove distractions. Remove things that cause you to be sidetracked from your goal.

Get help when you need it. If you need others to help, to give ideas, to solve problems with you, don't hesitate to draw them in. Don't miss a deadline because you avoided asking for help.

HAVING PATIENCE IN THE UNFOLDING OF EVENTS

'To every thing there is a season, and a time to every purpose under the heaven:

A time to be born, and a time to die; a time to plant, a time to reap that which is planted;

A time to kill, and a time to heal; a time to break down, and a time to build up;

A time to weep, and a time to laugh; a time to mourn, and a time to dance;

A time to cast away stones, and a time to gather stones together; a time to embrace, and a time to refrain from embracing;

A time to get, and a time to lose; a time to keep, and a time to cast away;

A time to rend, and a time to sew; a time to keep silence, and a time to speak;

A time to love, and a time to hate; a time of war, and a time of peace.'
– Ecclesiastes 3: 1–8

Patience can be challenging to develop and maintain in a world where everything is available now – fast food, fast communication, instant shopping and instant results. Often, we are trying to get somewhere, rush an outcome or make the unknown known.

With mindfulness, patience is the understanding that things develop in their own time, that life is a process of unfolding. There's a time for everything and everything takes time.

In Practice

'Patience is a form of wisdom. It demonstrates that we understand and accept the fact that sometimes things must unfold in their own time.'
– Jon Kabat-Zinn

Slow down to experience the unfolding of your life. Set and maintain the right pace of life that suits you. Being on a tight schedule or multi-tasking can lead to impatience. Being too busy is synonymous with impatience. Identify triggers that make you feel impatient. Make a list of them. Now reflect on why these situations make you feel impatient. What's the underlying cause of the feeling?

Practise being patient. Do one activity every day for a week that requires patience and record your progress. It could be a large jigsaw puzzle, sewing, knitting or embroidery, mending or constructing something. Decorate a room. Plant some tulip and daffodil bulbs. Whatever you choose, notice that, little by little, it comes into being – it comes about and is completed.

Practise being comfortable with sitting, doing nothing. When you have to wait, do you become impatient or uncomfortable? Instead of reading or getting your phone out or huffing and puffing, try just sitting there, looking around, taking in your surroundings. Try standing in line and just watching and listening to the people around you.

MANAGING DISTRACTIONS

'You can always find a distraction if you're looking for one.' – Tom Kite

Whether they're emails, text messages, social media, surfing the Internet or someone stopping by your desk for a chat, distractions take you away from what you are meant to be doing.

A distraction can be anything that diverts your attention, that you allow yourself to be attracted to. A distraction is a pleasant diversion. It can either come from yourself – something you're attracted to doing – or it can come as an interruption from someone else.

There's a difference, though, between an interruption and a distraction. Simply put, if you are driving your car, a red traffic light is an interruption. If you choose to take a detour, it's a distraction.

Distractions take away your focus from what you were doing for a longer period of time than an interruption. Distractions often need a lot of energy and effort to get you back to your main task.

And when distractions take up too much of your time and prevent you from getting your work done, it creates more stress for you and makes you more frustrated at work. But distractions are in your control.

In Practice

'Work is hard. Distractions are plentiful. And time is short.' – Adam Hochschild

Anticipate distractions. Only you know what they are and only you can avoid, manage or minimize them. If it's your phone or emails, turn them off. If it's other people, go somewhere where they can't waylay you. If it's your environment, put headphones on and listen to music to stay focused. Think ahead to what could be a distraction and try to distance yourself from it.

Anticipate your needs before you do something that needs your focus – whether you will need particular information, resources or just something to drink, get what you need and you'll be less likely to need to get out of your seat and lose focus.

Train yourself. Practise focus and engagement by turning off all distractions and committing your attention to a single task for a short amount of time (maybe 15 or 30 minutes) and work up to longer periods of time. As much as possible, do it when you know distractions are at a minimum.

Fiddle. Some people need to be *doing* something physical in order to focus their mind and divert themselves from other distractions. If you're one of these people, get something to fiddle with: worry beads, a bracelet, an elastic band, a squashy ball etc.

Stay motivated. If you feel tempted by a distraction, tell yourself that you will get to it in your break. But not sooner. Remind yourself what and why you're doing this and build in rewards.

Any time you realize you've allowed yourself to be distracted, don't berate yourself, just return to the task at hand. 'I know I lost focus, but I'm going to continue with what I'm doing now.'

BEING THANKFUL

'Hem your blessings with thankfulness so they don't unravel.' – Unknown

Gratitude, like mindfulness, is a way of noticing and relating to life. Gratitude typifies mindfulness. It involves being aware and acknowledging the positive things in your life.

Instead of appreciating what you have, it's easy to be dissatisfied and focus on what you haven't or what's 'wrong' with your life.

As the Tibetan saying goes, 'The moment we are content, we have enough. The problem is that we think the other way round, that we will be content only when we have enough.'

Even if you get to the end of the day feeling that not much went right, gratitude helps you see life through a positive lens. It turns what you do have into enough.

Just pausing to identify what you are thankful for can have a positive impact. When you focus your attention on the positive things, events and people in your life right now, you encourage your own happiness and well-being.

The smallest things in life can make the biggest difference too. Much of life is made up of small things and moments, one thing following another. Gratitude happens best when you notice the small pleasures around you, the things that often go unnoticed or unappreciated. It helps put everything into perspective and brings you into the moment.

And, during difficult and challenging times when you feel sad, frustrated or fearful, gratitude can be transformative. Appreciating even one little thing – like the sound of the rain, a good cup of tea or the comfort of your bed – can help reassure you.

In Practice

'Be thankful for what you have and you will end up with more.' – Oprah Winfrey

At the end of each day, identify three good things that have happened during that day. You may want to write them down in a notebook or simply reflect on what those things are while you're brushing your teeth.

Appreciate knowing that you had good in your day so that, whatever the other difficulties, you did, in fact, have things that made it all worthwhile. Instead of dwelling on the negative, get into the habit of noticing and reflecting on the small pleasures – what was good and right – instead. It could simply be that you had something good to eat, that the sun shone or that you received a supportive message from someone.

Think about a person or service for whom you are grateful. Notice what the people around you say and what they do and thank them. Express your gratitude to one person during the day. Tell them what you noticed or how they made a positive difference.

If you don't *know* that something has benefited you, you won't feel gratitude. So, the next time you pay a bill, think of something positive that the service or product has helped you achieve. This can shift your focus from thinking about what you had to give to what you receive.

Actively look for things to appreciate. After a while, it will become second nature.

GIVING COMPLIMENTS

'Too often we underestimate the power of ... an honest compliment, or the smallest act of caring, all of which have the potential to turn a life around.'
– Leo Buscaglia

You've probably experienced what it feels like when someone else says something nice to you. A simple compliment can brighten your day and make you feel good about yourself.

Compliments are a mark of mindful awareness. Why? Because to give a compliment you first have to be aware and acknowledge – to actively look for and comment on – other people's efforts and good intentions.

When you give praise, show appreciation or simply say 'thank you', your remarks let the other person know that their actions have been noticed.

Because compliments make the world a better place, everyone should learn how to compliment. You don't need to worry about getting the wording just right. You just need to keep in mind that a genuine sentiment phrased a bit awkwardly is better than saying nothing at all.

Compliments are gifts. They are not asked for or demanded. You don't need to be an expert to do it well. You just need to be honest and genuine.

In Practice

'Compliment people. Magnify their strengths, not their weaknesses.'
– Unknown

Be specific. The most memorable compliments are often the most specific ones, because it shows that you noticed. For example, 'The way you handled that question at the meeting was perfect. You totally refocused the discussion.'

Acknowledge personal qualities or special efforts. For example, 'Your calmness and patience really helped the situation.'

Explain why they made a difference. People feel good if they know that they made a difference. 'Your composure reassured me and everyone else.'

Put it in writing. Putting it in writing shows even more effort on your part while also giving the person a permanent reminder of the praise.

Make a positive comment on a website or blog. The next time you read something that really encourages or motivates you, let them know. Let someone know how they helped or inspired you with their book, website or blog. Write a positive review or comment.

Notice what someone is wearing and how they look. Compliments (appropriate compliments) on appearance make people feel good.

Notice the work someone does. It could be someone who serves you in a shop or café. It could be something about someone's business or someone in your office. Make a positive comment about their work or business.

Praise a parent for their child. There are few compliments more gratifying than when someone praises your child. When the opportunity arises, compliment someone on the abilities or behaviour of their child.

COOKING AND CONNECTING WITH FOOD

'You can usually cook something very good. Sometimes it is the only worthwhile product you can salvage from a day; what you make to eat.'
– John Irving

Where is your mind when you're cooking?

Are you going back over the day's events or perhaps you're thinking through your plans for the next day as you put the rice or pasta on? Perhaps you feel that at the end of the day preparing and making a meal is just one more chore, one more demand on your time.

And yet preparing and cooking can be meditative. Cooking provides an opportunity to be present, mindful and aware, as opposed to being distracted, stressed or overwhelmed.

Cooking is an opportunity to understand what it means to be in the here and now, with a sense of patience and appreciation, an opportunity to connect with the food that you eat.

Once you understand how to cook mindfully, you can repeat the experience every time you prepare and cook a meal.

In Practice

'I cook with wine. Sometimes I even add it to the food.' – W. C. Fields

Connect with nature's cycles and the passing of time. Use seasonal foods. Visit www.eattheseasons.co.uk or read Paul Waddington's book *Seasonal Food: A guide to what's in season when and why.*

Cook purposely and deliberately. With every ingredient you use, appreciate what's going into creating the meal. Look at your ingredients. Focus on the feel of the food in your hands.

Notice how the addition of each new ingredient affects the smells and sounds of the dish. Be present to the sights, sounds and smells of the food as it cooks. Taste as you go. Taste the raw vegetables (but not the meat!) the ingredients from the can, bottle, etc. and then continue to taste and sample a dish throughout the cooking process to see how flavours change. Breathe in the aroma of what you are cooking. Know that stirring food in a pan can be meditative.

When you've finished preparing and placed the food in the oven, under the grill or on the hob, sit in a chair not too far from the oven or hob and relax. You have nothing to do but be aware of the changing sounds and smells.

Try it just for a few minutes at a time. If your mind wanders off while you're doing this, as soon as you realize it's wandered, just bring your attention back to your senses, the sounds, the smell and the warmth of the room.

Adopt a beginner's mind and get out of mindless eating ruts. Try new food and recipes.

BANISHING BOREDOM

'Is life not a thousand times too short for us to bore ourselves?'
– Friedrich Nietzsche

When you start a new job, to one extent or another, you learn new things, meet new people and do new tasks.

But even the most exciting job can go a bit stale after a while. Once you get comfortable, it's easy to switch to autopilot, follow the same routines and get bored. Needless paperwork, pointless meetings, meaningless tasks, tedious routines, lack of interesting challenges and time spent waiting for other people to come through with information or resources: these are some of the boring activities many of us are faced with in the workplace.

Right now, you may have to stay in this job. Family commitments, proximity to where you work and financial concerns can often keep you stuck in a job that's boring. Is there anything you can do to stop boredom from dominating your work life when it may not be currently possible to change your job? Yes, there is. It involves finding ways to engage your mind.

In Practice

'I don't know where I'm going from here, but I promise it won't be boring.'
– David Bowie

Approach your situation with a beginner's mind. Your brain needs stimulating, so vary your routine. Inject new thinking into your work and mix things up a bit. Whatever you have to do, think of different ways to do it. For example, change the times you have your breaks or change the order in which you do things. Start the day with a different task, make your calls in the morning and don't check emails for two hours. Try doing your work at a different desk. And so on. Just think of the little things you could change to break up the daily routine.

Think about what specifically makes your job boring and look for ways to improve it. For example, if you're filing paperwork all afternoon, listening to music while you work could help.

Seek advice from others who aren't bored on the job – what do they find engages them?

Help out. It can refresh your outlook on your work and the aspects of it that bore you to involve different people. Ask other people whether you can help them with an aspect of their job.

Volunteer for everything that will make your job less tedious. If someone is off sick, offer to help do their job. Make sure it doesn't appear that you're trying to take over, though!

Learn new skills. Seek training to give you more skills to apply at work or that could lead to different work.

# MANAGING MOMENTS OF LONELINESS

'Only the lonely know how I feel tonight.' – Roy Orbison

Loneliness is not the same as being alone. To be alone simply means to be physically separate from others. But loneliness is an emotional state. It's a feeling of isolation or separation.

Loneliness is something that most of us experience from time to time. You may experience loneliness as a vague feeling that something is not right, a kind of emptiness. Or you may feel loneliness as deprivation and pain.

There are all sorts of reasons why you may feel lonely and cut off from others. Divorce, bereavement, mental or physical health problems, disability, discrimination, unemployment and being a carer are all common causes of loneliness. And although moving to a new area, starting a new job or having a baby can be exciting and positive, people often find that new experiences can leave them feeling lonely.

You may have lots of social contact or be in a relationship or part of a family and still feel lonely.

Whatever the circumstances, the common experience is a feeling of being disconnected. You feel sad, alone and that either no one understands or that they misunderstand. Typically, when you're lonely, your mind shifts to ruminative cycles of the past and future that lend themselves to disconnection, leading to more loneliness.

But it is possible to manage loneliness. Mindfulness can help you to see that a sense of connection is always available to you, whatever your circumstances.

In Practice

'I wandered lonely as a cloud / That floats on high o'er vales and hills'
– William Wordsworth

Take up a hobby. Social contact and friendships are not the only way to feel connected. Activities like gardening, reading, drawing, yoga, swimming and cycling can help you feel engaged and connected. If you have a hobby or passion that you can lose yourself in, you will even find yourself searching out moments to be by yourself in order to write, read, paint, bake, garden, cycle etc.

These activities leave no room for undesirable thoughts. As you focus on what's happening and what you're doing, the merging of activity and thoughts keeps you fully absorbed in the moment.

Make the most of opportunities for social contact. Find others like you. Find out where the other knitters, singers, hikers or kite-boarders are. Go to www.meetup.com. Connect with them through your shared interests. Regular meetings will also provide some structure in your life so that you have things to look forward to.

Get support. Whatever the reason for your situation, you can find a group that provides information, support and opportunities to share experiences with other people in a similar situation.

Make a contribution. If you're feeling lonely, reach out. If you can help other people, in the process you help yourself. Even helping just one person is a start. It will take the focus away from you. Volunteer for a cause. It will help you in meeting people who feel strongly about something and with whom you can make a genuine connection.

Think about getting a pet. Consider adopting a dog or cat from your local animal shelter. The trust and affection of an animal can create a connection between you. As someone once said, 'Cats and dogs are very good at something that humans aren't: living in the present.'

PERFORMING SPONTANEOUS ACTS OF KINDNESS

'Ask yourself: Have you been kind today? Make kindness your daily modus operandi and change your world.' – Annie Lennox

Kindness is related to compassion. With compassion, the focus is on the alleviation of suffering. Kindness, on the other hand, is simply concerned with people being considerate and showing goodwill towards others. Acts of kindness are selfless acts that either assist or lift the spirits of someone else. There need be no reason to be kind other than to make people smile, or be happier.

Kindness is mindful. It takes you out of yourself. You have to be aware, to actively look for opportunities in the present moment to be kind. Kind gestures free you from focusing on yourself and enable you to reach out to someone else.

You may feel you have little to offer, but whether it is a smile, a cup of tea, an invitation to dinner or an offer to help carry something, it is the act of giving itself that is important. As Gandhi said, 'Almost anything we do will seem insignificant, but it is very important that we do it.'

Of course, some people are easy to be kind to. If they show gratitude or if they have been kind to you first, it's easier to be kind back.

It's not, though, easy to be kind when you're wound up or stressed. It's not easy to be kind to people who are rude. But keep in mind that although they may not be nice, you are. And if you can show a kindness it can make you both feel better.

In Practice

'Carry out a random act of kindness, with no expectation of reward, safe in the knowledge that one day someone may do the same for you.' – Diana, Princess of Wales

Start your day by sending an email specifically designed to help someone else. Make introductions, send some encouragement or offer a helpful resource or link.

Reach out to someone you haven't talked to in a while. Today, take a few minutes to reconnect with someone. Write them a card, email or text to let them know you were thinking about them.

Smile at people. Smile at people you pass in the street, in a queue, to the person who serves you in a shop or café.

Tip big. Give a tip that makes the waiter's day.

Be polite on the road. Be kind to other drivers. In a queue, when a driver tries to merge into your lane, let them in with a smile.

Treat someone to cake. It could be your colleagues, neighbours family or friends. Whoever you choose, surprise them by bringing in a homemade or shop-bought cake. In the summer, bring in some fresh fruit – strawberries or melon.

Save a life. Donate blood. Donated blood is a lifeline for many people needing long-term treatments, not just in emergencies. Your blood's main components – red cells, plasma and platelets – are vital for many different uses. Go to http://www.blood.co.uk.

Speak kindly. Practise speaking in a kind way. And every time you do have a negative thought, counter it aloud with a positive one.

FOCUSING AND ENGAGING YOUR ATTENTION

'If you don't know where you are going, you will probably end up some-where else.' – Laurence J. Peter

Mindfulness requires focus: a clear and defined point of attention. It means managing your attention so that it is focused and occupied with immediate experience.

Often, the advice is to quiet your mind for ten minutes and focus on a breathing meditation to help you find inner peace, calm and balance.

But it's not easy to simply sit and meditate – to quiet your mind and focus on your breathing – without your mind wandering.

There is, though, a way to keep effortlessly focused for relatively long periods, to be 'in the zone'. It's known as 'flow'.

'Flow' refers to time spent doing something that keeps you focused and engaged.

If you have ever started a job or activity and become so absorbed in what you were doing that time passed without you noticing, you were in a flow state of mind. You thought of nothing else as you concentrated and focused, your awareness merged with the activity and you were 'living in the moment'.

With flow activities, your mind is fully occupied with one activity. It's unlikely your mind will wander, as it is immersed in a feeling of positive focus and enjoyment in the process of the activity. Thoughts and emotions are not just contained and channelled: they are positive, energized and aligned with the task at hand.

The level of engagement absorbs you so deeply, keeping attention so focused, that nothing can distract you. It's as though a water current is effortlessly carrying you along.

In Practice

'Life is short. Focus on what matters and let go of what doesn't.' – Unknown

Identify the things you enjoy doing: hobbies, sports, interests. They are activities where you can experience flow. If you can't think of anything that you currently do, start something new. Here're some ideas to get you started:

- **Play a sport.** Badminton, squash, tennis or table tennis, rugby or football, bowling or billiards. Whatever it is, everything in sport happens in the moment. Yoga, boxing and judo, darts and archery, rock climbing, canoeing and swimming are just a few examples of flow activities. Focusing on each individual movement forces your mind to live in that single moment with your body.
- **Sing and dance to music.** Join a dance class, be it ballet, ballroom, hip hop or tap.
- **Join a choir.** Sing and dance along to your favourite tunes in the kitchen. You'll become immersed in the music and really be in the moment.
- **Take up a hobby.** Gardening, cooking, painting, drawing, calligraphy, crochet, woodcarving, model building, juggling, whatever it is, for many people a creative activity is a place to dwell happily in the present moment.
- **Start playing an instrument.** Piano, guitar, drums, flute or harmonica, whatever it is, for many people, playing an instrument is a mindful meditation in itself.
- **Play games and puzzles.** Whether they're card or board games, computer games, jigsaws, crosswords or Sudoku, all require a level of concentration and provide a challenge that will have you totally absorbed.
- **Read a book or watch a film.** It could be a gripping thriller, science fiction or a clever comedy. Whatever the genre, a good book or film can capture your attention completely.

MANAGING CHANGE

'Change is inevitable – except from a vending machine.' – Robert C. Gallagher

We may not know how or when change is going to show up in our lives, but one thing is for sure: it *will* show up. And it's not always welcome. Whether it's redundancy, your children growing up and leaving home, your favourite restaurant changing the menu or your town centre streets being turned into a one-way system, changes are never far from your door.

Too often, we resist strange new situations and circumstances. We fight to hold onto people, places and things. We struggle to let go.

But when you resist change, you are simply clinging to the past and fearful of the future.

Of course, not all change is unwelcome – when you get the job, buy the house you want, travel somewhere new and interesting. It's at times like this you notice what you have to gain from change.

The question is, 'How can you manage change when it's unwelcome and – as far as you can see – uncalled for?'

Mindfulness can help by helping you to let go and accept the new situation, to keep an open mind and accept it will take time to adjust.

Mindfulness can help you to see that everything comes to pass. Nothing comes to stay.

In Practice

'God, grant me the serenity to accept the things I cannot change, courage to change the things I can and wisdom to know the difference.'
– Reinhold Niebuhr

Embrace change by seeking change. By changing even small routines, you can train your mind to accommodate changes. Changing the things you *do* can change the way you *think*.

Move the clock or bin to a different place in the room. Or move the teabags, jam or cereal to a different cupboard in the kitchen. See how often you automatically look for these items in the place they used to be. Confusing? Frustrating? Yes. But you can adjust. After only a couple of weeks, you will have adjusted to the changes.

Then try these:

- Cook a new recipe.
- Listen to new music or a different radio station.
- Walk or drive a new route to work.
- Change how you travel – walk instead of cycle. Cycle instead of drive. Or get public transport. Take the stairs instead of the lift.

Try new activities and experiences that encourage your mind to be open to new possibilities.

Accept change. When change is foisted upon you, recognize and accept that you cannot control what has already happened. But you can see change as an opportunity. Find the benefit in the change. There's always a benefit and an opportunity.

Be patient. Wherever you are within a process of change, allow yourself time to adjust. What could be more futile than resisting what already is? Once you accept a change, rather than react to it – take impulsive, opposing action – you can respond to it – act thoughtfully and favourably.

KNOWING WHEN TO START OVER

'Everybody's got a past. The past doesn't equal the future unless you live there.'
– Tony Robbins

When it comes to leaving a miserable job, calling time on an unhappy relationship or ditching joyless exercise classes, too often many of us simply decide to stay the course.

Why can't you let go and move on? Perhaps you can't see an alternative. Often, it's difficult to walk away if you can't see another path to take, especially if walking away could mean quite a big change in your life.

Maybe you feel you've made a commitment and so should stick with it and put up with the difficulties. Perhaps you don't want to admit that you were wrong to have put up with a bad situation for so long. Anyway, you're so used to it, you may as well carry on.

You're probably thinking about the sunk costs: the time, effort, love or money you have already put in and can never get back.

But sunk costs can fool you into sticking with something. You continue to put more time, effort or money into someone or something even though it's plainly not doing you any good.

Of course, you don't want to give up too easily on your commitments, but refusing to let go of something that's making you miserable means you are allowing your past to dictate your present.

Don't keep making the same mistake. Know that strength shows in your ability not only to persist but also to start over, to let go of the past and begin again in the present.

In Practice

'No matter how filled up your canvas of life seems to be, in reality it's always blank, every moment is a blank page. It seems convoluted with words, texts and storyline, but in reality it's a blank page.' – Bentinho Massaro

Let go. Realize that at the time, based on what you knew and how you felt, you did make the right choice. At the time, your decision *was* the right one. Now though, the situation isn't right for you.

Feel better about your mistake. Find something positive about the situation. However bad the situation, you can always draw something good out.

Start again. Beginner's mind encourages you to respond to things as they are right now. Think about what you have to gain from the moment you let go, rather than what you have to lose by pulling out. All that matters is which option will be the best from this moment on.

Identify what you've learnt from the experience and what you will do differently now. Think about what you've learnt about yourself as a result of this experience. Keep an open mind on how to apply your experience to your current situation.

Be patient. Know that if you pull out of the relationship, the job or university course now, although it will take time to adjust, you will have less anxiety and stress and more control over your life.

If you can't see an alternative way forward, talk to friends, family and colleagues and ask for their ideas. Seek professional advice if you need information from an expert.

If your commitment was to someone else, let them down gently and, if it helps, suggest a way that you could make up for it.

CONCLUSION

You may have started this book at the beginning and read right through to the end. I imagine, though, that you have dipped in and out. You probably turned to the themes and situations that most interest you first and then read through some of the other pages.

Whichever way you've been reading this book, you'll see that you can, in fact, start anywhere. As the poet Kabir said, 'Wherever you are that's the entry point.' You can start at any point in your day and in any part of your life, in anything you do and with anything that you think about.

Mindfulness isn't a set of instructions. It's simply a framework of guiding principles to help provide perspective, focus and calm progress in the big events in your life and the ordinary everyday moments and activities – the comings and goings of your daily life.

Having read this book, you will, I hope, be clear that mindfulness is not something limited to Buddhists, mystics, academics or psychologists. Mindfulness is a simple process that anyone can do.

It's not always easy, though. Often, you have to remind yourself to be mindful. So, whatever you have or haven't read so far, do make sure you read the first chapter: 'Creating a Mindfulness Habit'.

And, at any one time, when you recognize that you are being (or have been) mindful – that you've been aware, acknowledged and accepted what's happened, that you've been focused and engaged or that you've let go of the past and adopted a beginner's mind – be aware how you got there and recreate it as often as possible.

Be the most mindful version of you!

ABOUT THE AUTHOR

Gill Hasson is a teacher, trainer and writer. She has 20 years' experience in the area of personal development. Her expertise is in the areas of confidence and self-esteem, communication skills, assertiveness and resilience.

Gill delivers teaching and training for educational organizations, voluntary and business organizations and the public sector.

Gill is the author of the bestselling *Mindfulness* and *Emotional Intelligence* plus other books on the subjects of dealing with difficult people, resilience, communication skills and assertiveness.

Gill's particular interest and motivation is in helping people to realize their potential, to live their best life! You can contact Gill via her website www.gillhasson.co.uk or email her at gillhasson@btinternet.com.

MORE MINDFUL QUOTES AND SAYINGS

'Like your body, your mind also gets tired so refresh it by wise sayings.' – Hazrat Ali

'Begin doing what you want to do now. We are not living in eternity. We have only this moment, sparkling like a star in our hand – and melting like a snowflake.' – Francis Bacon

'Emancipate yourself from mental slavery. None but ourselves can free our mind.' – Bob Marley

'Learn from yesterday, live for today, hope for tomorrow.' – Albert Einstein

'The only happiness found on top of the mountain is the happiness you bring up there.' – Unknown

'For things to reveal themselves to us, we need to be ready to abandon our views about them.' – Thich NhẫHạnh

'Mindfulness is the ultimate mobile device; you can use it anywhere, anytime, unobtrusively.' – Sharon Salzberg

'Life is just like an old time rail journey ... delays, sidetracks, smoke, dust, cinders, and jolts, interspersed only occasionally by beautiful vistas and thrilling bursts of speed. The trick is to thank the Lord for letting you have the ride.' – Gordon B. Hinckley

'My happiness grows in direct proportion to my acceptance and in inverse proportion to my expectations.' – Michael J. Fox

'I'm less interested in why we're here. I'm wholly devoted to while we're here.' – Erika Harris